PETER MAYLE

A Dog's Life

Peter Mayle's previous books include *A Year in Provence, Toujours Provence,* and *Hotel Pastis.* His most recent book is *Anything Considered.*

Boy was found abandoned on the outskirts of a village in Provence. Having landed on his feet, he now divides his time between the kitchen and the forest.

A Dog's Life

A Dog's Life

PETER MAYLE

With drawings by
Edward Koren

Vintage Books
A Division of Random House, Inc.   *New York*

FIRST VINTAGE BOOKS EDITION, JUNE 1996

The Library of Congress has cataloged
the Knopf edition as follows:
Mayle, Peter.
A dog's life / by Peter Mayle;
with drawings by Edward Koren.—1st ed.
p. cm.
ISBN 0-679-44122-0
1. Dogs—France—Provence—Fiction.
2. Human-animal relationships—France—Provence—Fiction.
3. Provence (France)—Fiction. I. Title.
PT6063.A8875D64 1995
823'.914—dc20 94-42590
CIP
Vintage ISBN: 0-679-76267-1

Author photograph © Jennie Mayle

Random House Web address: http://www.randomhouse.com/

Printed in the United States of America
10 9 8 7 6 5 4 3 2 1

To Jean-Claude Ageneau,
Dominique Roizard, and Jonathan Turetsky,
three princes among vets

AUTHOR'S NOTE

My story is based on actual events. However, following the current autobiographical custom adopted by politicians in their memoirs, I have adjusted the truth wherever it might reflect unfavorably on myself.

A Dog's Life

Destiny, Celebrity, Proust, and Me

*L*ife is unfair, as we all know, and a good thing, too. If it had gone according to plan, I would still be chained up outside some farmhouse in the middle of nowhere, living on short rations and barking at the wind. But fortunately, some of us are marked by fate to overcome humble beginnings and succeed in a competitive world. Lassie comes to mind, for instance, and that small creature who seems to spend his entire life with his head at an unnatural angle, listening to an antique gramophone. Rather him than me, but I suppose there's not a great choice for terriers—noisy little brutes with limited intelligence, in my experience.

As my memoirs unfold, I shall describe my progress through life in more detail—all the way from birth to my present eminence, not forgetting the times of struggle, the months in the wilderness, house hunting, curious encounters, milestones, turning points, and so on. But for the moment, let us put these aside and turn to more fundamental matters: my emergence as a celebrity and my decision to air my views in print.

It started, as these things often do, by chance. A photographer had come to the house, looking for a free drink under the pretext of doing artistic studies of the lavender patch. I didn't pay him too much attention, apart from a cursory sniff, but he put down his glass long enough to take a few informal portraits. I was in silhouette, I remember, with the sun behind me—*contre-jour,* as we say in France—and I heard him muttering something about the noble savage as I stopped to water a geranium.

At the time, I thought no more of it. Some of us

A chance encounter

Star quality

are photogenic, and some aren't. But a few weeks later, there I was in a magazine: full color, whiskers bristling, tail upthrust—the living essence of the fearless guard dog. And they say the camera never lies. Little do they know.

After that, it never stopped. Other magazines, or at least, those with the wit to recognize star quality, came to seek me out. Newspapers, television crews, various admirers from near and far and a furtive couple trying to sell out-of-date dog food—they all turned up, and I did my best to fit them in. And then the letters started to arrive.

I don't know if you've ever received a letter from a complete stranger asking about your personal habits; I must have had hundreds of them, and quite impertinent some of them were, too. I was even offered safe sex with a rottweiler (no such thing, if you ask me, not with those jaws). Anyway, it soon became obvious that the world was waiting for some kind of message from me—a statement of principles, perhaps, or what is known nowadays as a "lifestyle guide." I brooded on this.

Now, over the years, I have developed a soft spot for Proust. He tends to go on a bit for my taste, but we do have several characteristics in common. Both French, of course. Both with a reflective nature. Both keen admirers of the biscuit—madeleines for him, and the calcium-enriched, bone-shaped, extra - crunchy model for me. And so, I thought to myself, if he can share his opinions about life, love, his mother, teatime treats, and the pursuit of happiness, why can't I? Not that I remember my mother too well, actually, because she left very shortly after having me and the other twelve. Given the circumstances, I can't say I blame her, although it put quite a strain on my faith in the maternal instinct at the time. Those were dark and thirsty days indeed, as you'll see.

But I digress. Literature beckons, and I must try to arrange my thoughts. On the whole, it has been a charmed life, despite my underprivileged beginnings. The patron saint of dogs—St. Bernard, for those of you who don't know—has been good to me. Even so, experience has caused me to form certain

Literature beckons

opinions, and readers of a sensitive disposition may be offended by the odd remarks about babies, cats, hygiene, poodles, and vets who insist on taking one's temperature the old-fashioned way. For these candid comments, I offer no apologies. What use are journals such as this if they don't reveal the author, warts and all?

In Trouble

There were far too many at my birthday party, and I wouldn't have invited any of them. I couldn't see them at first, because it takes a few days for the eyes to open, but they made their presence felt. Try having breakfast with a football team, all of them fighting to get hold of the same piece of toast, and you'll know what I went through. Pandemonium, every man for himself, elbows everywhere, and to hell with table manners. Being young at the time, of course, I couldn't imagine that it would cause problems, apart from some bumping and boring at mealtimes. How wrong I was.

There were thirteen of us altogether, and limited outlets at the maternal bosom. The trouble was that mother had been taken by surprise—first by my father behind the barn and then by our arrival in such numbers, when she was only equipped to cater for half a dozen at a time. Obviously, this meant separate sittings every few hours. She was always complaining about lack of sleep, puppy rash, and postnatal depression. Looking back, I'm not surprised.

You hear all kinds of nonsense these days about the plight of the only child. People prattle on in their concerned way about loneliness, lack of sibling contact, too much attention from the parents, quiet and solitary meals, and all the rest of it. Sounds like heaven to me, absolute heaven. Rather that any day than having to go ten rounds against a dozen opponents with chronic milk lust every time you feel peckish. It wears you out, and plays havoc with the digestion. Large families should be restricted to rabbits. I feel sure Proust would agree with me here.

And that's what my poor, weary mother must have felt, too, because no sooner were we all more or less on our feet and blinking at the world than she disappeared. Just like that. I remember the moment well. Dead of night, it was, and I was half-asleep. I rolled over for a little sustenance, as one does, and woke up sucking hard on my brother's ear. It gave us both quite a shock, as a matter of fact, and he looked at me sideways for some time afterward. I'd be interested to know what the sibling-contact enthusiasts would have recommended in that situation; group therapy, no doubt, with a session of self-awareness training and a stiff shot of antibiotics for the injured party.

None of us got much sleep for the rest of that night, as you can imagine, and by morning stomachs were rumbling, with the weaker brethren starting to wail. Being an optimist, I felt sure that mother dear had just slipped out for a little adult company behind the barn and would be back with a smirk on her face in time for breakfast.

But not a bit of it. The hours passed, the rumbling and wailing grew louder, and even I began to fear the worst. Motherless, surrounded by a bunch of ninnies, still with the faint taste of the fraternal ear in my mouth and no immediate prospect of anything more nourishing, it was my first experience of the darker side of life.

I've often wondered how we scraped through the next few weeks. The lord and lady of the household distributed the odd bowl of thin milk and some decidedly secondhand scraps (to this day, I can't work up any interest in cold noodles), but it was poor, unsatisfactory stuff. Even so, you'd think they were giving us top-grade sirloin, from the fuss they made. Each day, I'd see them arguing outside the barn door, she in her carpet slippers and he wearing boots. Some of it escaped me, but I didn't care much for the general drift. Too many mouths to feed, money down the drain, it can't go on like this; something must be done; it's all your fault for letting her out of the house at full moon—I've never heard so much heated debate about the distribution of a few old chicken bones and half a baguette that had seen better days. But it was that or nothing, so we made do.

Then we began to receive visitors, and the old hypocrite in the boots changed his tune. He'd bring his friends in to look at us, and he would talk about us as though we were family heirlooms. "Prime hunting stock," he'd say, "from a long line of champions. Impeccable genes. You can tell from the shape of the head and the beautifully turned withers." Needless to say, he was making it all up. I'd lay odds he hadn't even seen my father; I never had. But on and on he went, tossing in comments about distinguished pedigrees and bloodlines that went back to the days of Louis XIV. It was a performance that would have brought a blush to the cheek of a used-car salesman.

Most of his friends saw through it, but there are always a few simpletons around, and one by one my siblings were bundled off to new homes, passed off as purebred hunting dogs. It just goes to show what you can get away with if you're a shameless bluffer. It's a lesson I took to heart, and it has served me well many times. I remember the day I met a family of wild boar in the forest, for instance, but that's another story.

You may wonder how I felt as I watched those near and dear to me leaving the ancestral home. Bereft, perhaps? Lonely and glum? Not exactly. There's good and bad in every situation, and it didn't take me long to work out that fewer mouths to feed means more for those who remain. Heartless and self-centered, you may say, but an empty stomach changes your view of life. Besides, I always considered myself to be the pick of the litter—if you had seen the others you would understand why—and so I was confident that I would one day assume my rightful role in the scheme of things, with three square meals a day and a comfortable bunk indoors. We can all make mistakes.

I started to pay closer attention to the one in the boots, as he was clearly in charge, and I used to flatter the miserable scoundrel every time he came within range. My technique wasn't as polished then as it is now, but I did as best I could with the agitated tail and the squeals of delight, and I was misguided enough to feel that I was making headway. Somewhere beneath that unattractive exterior, I thought, was a kindly soul who would eventually warm to me. Alas, there was less to him than met the eye. You've probably heard that description of life as being nasty, brutish, and short. Well, there you have him. Too free with his boots, even then, which is why I've had a profound distrust of feet ever since.

But one day, he let me out of the barn, and I thought that life was taking a turn for the better. I anticipated an outing at the very least, and maybe a tour of inspection of my new lodgings, with a decent meal to celebrate my arrival in the family home. Ah, the foolish optimism of youth.

He took me over to a scruffy patch of garden,

planted with weeds and rusty oil cans and a couple of
ancient tractor tires, slipped a noose over my head,
looped the other end of the rope around the trunk of
a plane tree, and then stood back and studied me. I
don't know if you've ever watched people trying to
decide between the lamb and the beef in a butcher's
shop, but that's how he looked—thoughtful and cal-
culating. I jumped up and down and performed a
modest frolic, almost throttling myself in the noose,
and then gave up and sat in the dust. We stared at
each other. He sucked his mustache. I tried a piteous
whimper. He grunted and went back into the house.
So much for the mystical communion between man
and dog.

And there I was for the duration of the summer—
tied up, bored, and badly fed, taking what comfort I
could from the shade of the plane tree. From time to
time, he'd come over and look me up and down in
that thoughtful way, but apart from that there was
very little in the way of diversion. I barked a great
deal, just for something to do, and watched ants.
Busy little fellows, ants. They still fascinate me,
rushing hither and yon, eyes front, in lines of three
abreast. Big cities are like that, so I hear, millions of
people going from one hole to another and then back
again. Odd way to live your life, but there it is.

I had taken to spending the night curled up in one
of the tractor tires, and one morning I woke up to
find a definite change in the air. It had the smell of a

different season about it, and there was a heavy dew on the rubber. Summer was over.

I know now, although I didn't then, that the start of autumn brings out the primitive urge that lurks in the breast of mankind, particularly in my part of the world. Men get together, arm themselves to the teeth, and go forth to do battle with thrushes, rabbits, snipe, or anything else that makes a suspicious sound in the bushes. It has been known for them to shoot each other, which is understandable if you've had a disappointing day with the rabbits and want something to take home to the wife. But I digress.

I had emerged from my tire, had a stretch, sniffed the breeze, and was expecting another dull day like any other when what I can only describe as an apparition came marching out of the house. It was the one in boots, and instead of his usual vest and moth-eaten trousers, he was arrayed in full jungle camouflage—mottled brown-and-green cap and matching jacket, bandolier of cartridges, a bag slung over one shoulder, a gun over the other, Nimrod the hunter in fancy dress.

As he came closer, I caught a whiff of stale blood from his bag—a great improvement, I may say, over the familiar bouquet of garlic, tobacco, and sweat— and I sensed that something was up. Sure enough, he untied me and indicated with his boot that I should join him in his van. I realize that this may not sound like the start of a perfect day to you, but I'd been on the end of that rope for months, and so you can imagine that I treated this as a great adventure. There's a limit to one's interest in ants, after all.

So off we went, leaving the road after a while to bump up a rough track before stopping. Nimrod got out but made me stay in the van. I heard barking and poked my nose through the window.

Three or four other vans, each with a dog inside, from the sound of it, were parked in a clearing of the forest. Nimrod and his friends were strutting about, clapping each other on the back in manly fashion and comparing armaments and military regalia. A bottle of something was produced and passed around, and one of the warriors took out a sausage, which was hacked up with a knife big enough to have gutted a whale and then consumed as if none of them had seen food for days. They'd only just had breakfast, too. Then there was more activity with the bottle, the barking died down, and I must have dozed off.

Next thing I remember was being pulled out of the van by my scruff and ordered into the forest. The other dogs seemed to know what to do, so I did the same. We put our noses to the ground and ran around in a purposeful way, with the armored division bringing up the rear. They were making enough noise to scare off anything that wasn't stone-deaf, and any bird with half a brain (your pheasant, for instance) would have taken off for a safe perch on the roof of the *gendarmerie* long before our arrival.

But you can never account for the behavior of rab-

Cowering under a bush was bunny.

bits. One of the other dogs suddenly stopped and adopted the pose that you see occasionally in paintings of the rustic school—head thrust forward, neck, spine, and tail in a perfect straight line, one front paw raised as if he'd stepped in something unpleasant. I think the technical term is *at point.* Anyway, I trotted over to see what was going on, and there, cowering under a bush, was bunny, shaking like jelly and clearly at a loss to know whether to roll over and play dead, put up the white flag, or make a run for it.

There was great excitement among the troops behind us, and various instructions were passed on, which I ignored. It was my first rabbit, after all, and I wanted to take a closer look. A decent lunch was in my mind, I remember, as I made a lunge for him, but he must have read my thoughts. He bolted through my legs, and then World War III broke out.

You must understand that I had never been in combat before, and so I wasn't prepared for the dreadful din of several guns going off within inches of my head. You have no idea what a shock it was to the system, and so I make no excuses for my actions. Instinct took over, and I got out of the firing line faster than the rabbit. In fact, I think I may have overtaken him on the way back to the safety of the van.

I couldn't get in, so I dived underneath, and I was just getting my breath back and congratulating myself on a successful escape from the jaws of death when I became aware that I was no longer alone. I could hear the sound of laughter, and some ripe language that I recognized was coming from Nimrod. He was the only one who wasn't laughing.

He bellowed at me to come out, but I thought it best to stay put for the moment and let him regain his composure. He started kicking the side of the van, amid increased merriment from the other members of the party, and when that didn't work, he got down on all fours, poked me out with the butt of his gun, opened the door of the van, and helped me in with his boot.

The trip home wasn't a great social success. I knew I hadn't acquitted myself with quite the skill and dexterity expected of me, but it was, after all, my first time out. How was I supposed to know the rules of

The trip home wasn't a great social success.

the game? In the interests of harmony and a quiet
life, I tried making a few apologetic overtures, but
all I got was the back of his hand and a stream of
abuse. What I hadn't realized, of course, was that
I'd made him look like the cretin that he was in front
of his peers (who weren't much better, from the look
of them, but at least they had a sense of humor). People are touchy about how they see themselves, I've
discovered. One tiny crack in the mirror of self-
esteem, and they sulk for hours. Or they take out
their foul temper on the nearest available object—in
this case, me.

So it was back on the end of the rope and in disgrace for a few days while Nimrod and I considered our respective positions. He obviously wanted a hunting companion, steady with wing and shot. My ambitions were more in the domestic line, perhaps a little light guard duty and a roof over my head. Not that I object to hunting on moral grounds, you understand. As far as I'm concerned, a dead rabbit is easier to get to grips with than a mobile one. It's the noise of those guns I can't abide. I have extremely sensitive ears.

The final straw came a few days later, when Nimrod decided he would put me through some elementary dressage and field training. He came out of the house brandishing his gun and a shapeless bundle of fur—one of his terrible old vests, I think it was, rolled up, with a rabbit skin tied around it.

He slipped the rope from my neck and pushed the bundle under my nose for a few seconds, muttering something about the scent of the wild, forgetting that he'd been using the vest to wipe his hands on while he was tinkering with his van. It's not easy to work up any true excitement over a strong odor of diesel fuel, but I did my best to appear alert and keen, and then the next stage of the farce began.

He threw the bundle into a clump of high weeds twenty yards away, then put his hand down to prevent me from chasing it. I had no intention of going anywhere near it, in fact, not with a trigger-happy old lunatic behind me, and so I sat there awaiting developments. He seemed to take this as an act of exemplary restraint and field craft, and he leered at me in what I suppose he thought was a smile of approval. "*Bieng*," he said (he had an accent like soup), "*ça commence bieng*."

Now what? Were we going to wait for the vest and its fur coat to come out from the weeds and surrender to superior forces? Were we going to creep up on it and catch it unaware? While we were deciding what to do, I lay down, an error of judgment as it turned out, because it inhibits one's speed off the mark.

I wasn't even looking at him, so I never saw him raise the gun. But when it went off, I was away and into one of the tractor tires, head down and paws over ears, before you could say bang.

Have you ever seen a man completely lose control of himself? It's not a pretty sight, especially if he's waving a gun in your direction and gibbering with fury, so I thought I'd better put something solid between the two of us. With one bound, I was out of the tractor tire and behind the plane tree before he could get the rope back over my head. We went around and around the tree trunk several times, him cursing like a man possessed and me doing all I could to look suitably penitent while going backward at top speed. Not easy, I may say, but I thought it was safer than presenting the rear view, although he'd probably have missed that, not being much of a marksman.

It might have ended eventually in an exhausted truce had it not been for the arrival of one of his friends, who stood there with tears of laughter running down his face at the sight of us playing what must have looked like an energetic game of ring-around-the-tree-trunk. Now that I think of it, I'm sure it was the ridicule that was responsible for my subsequent change of address. You must have found that yourself: There are those among us who can't take a joke.

Events then moved quickly and rather painfully. Once he'd managed to corner me, he gave me a couple of stingers with the end of the rope and tossed me in the back of the van. I heard him shouting to his wife—what a cross she had to bear, poor old dear—before getting into the van, growling at me, and driving off as if he was late for his best friend's funeral and didn't want to miss the party.

I kept well out of the way, beyond reach in the back, and brooded. We weren't going hunting again, I could tell, because he didn't have his wretched gun and silly hat. It was equally obvious that this wasn't a pleasure excursion. He had a stiff, angry set to his head and shoulders, and he was driving much too fast for his limited powers of physical coordination, sounding his horn at all and sundry and lurching around corners like a one-legged drunk.

On and on we went, going uphill most of the time, until we came to a bumpy halt off the road. I braced myself for further unpleasantness, and when he got

out and came around to the back of the van, I slipped
into the driver's seat, just in case he had plans of a
violent nature in mind. We looked at each other, him
through the open rear door of the van, me over the
back of the seat.

We looked at each other.

I was half-expecting another chorus of bellowing,
but instead he reached in his pocket and produced a
sizable chunk of sausage, which he held out to me. I
should have known that a mean-spirited old villain
like him wouldn't suddenly become afflicted with
generosity, but I was hungry, you see, and taken by

surprise. So I followed the proferred sausage. He gradually moved backward from the van, and I jumped out and sat in my most appealing position, front paws together, head cocked, and digestive juices at the ready.

He nodded and grunted, then held the sausage under my nose. It was pork, I remember, with just the right amount of fat and a wonderfully spicy smell. But as I was leaning forward to take it, he turned and threw it into the bushes. A long throw it was, too, for someone who was always whimpering about his arthritis.

Well, I dare say you can guess what happened. I went after the sausage, thinking that this was exactly my kind of hunting, and dived into the undergrowth, nose working overtime and feeling that maybe things were looking up. The thrill of the chase must have taken over, because I wasn't conscious of any sound behind me. Also, I'm not what you'd call stealthy, and I was probably making a fair amount of noise getting through the vegetation. In any case, after ten minutes of fruitless casting around, I stopped to get my sense of direction, looked back, and saw that something was missing.

The landscape was bare: no van, no man. He'd gone while I was otherwise engaged. I never did find the sausage, either.

In Limbo

*A*bandoned—that was the word that came to mind eventually, after scanning the empty horizon for a glimpse of the van and its devious owner. I took it as a hint that my services were no longer required at Château Despair, and with no pressing appointments, I had plenty of time to take stock and ponder the future.

It was a turning point, no doubt about it, and what I've discovered about turning points is that they are what you make of them. There's good and bad, sunshine and shade, bitter and sweet, and so forth. Is the glass half-empty or half-full? Does every silver lining have a cloud? That sort of thing.

As I've mentioned, I'm an optimist by nature, and so I started by considering the bright side. I was free to roam wherever my nose took me. There was no immediate threat of a kick in the ribs, or earsplitting expeditions with a group of armed idiots. And my previous lodging and feeding arrangements, as you've seen, could hardly have been worse. To leave those behind was no hardship.

There was a problem, however, which began to intrude, in the way that problems do. Whatever other abilities I possessed, I was not equipped by nature to fend for myself. That's the difference between dogs and cats. My early experience with Hepzibah, which I'll describe later, had not endeared me to cats. Throw one of them out in the wilderness (and I have to admit I'd be the first to help), and before you know it he'd be tucking in to a thrush cutlet and making himself free with any nest or rabbit hole that took his fancy. In other words, he would have answered the call of the wild by going native and making a beast of himself. It's always there with cats, you know, that instinct. They're not to be trusted, and they have one or two disgusting personal habits, too, in my opinion, but that's by the way.

Ruminating on this, my thoughts turned to the position of the dog in what is loosely called "civilized society." I dare say you're familiar with the phrase that has been like a collar around our necks for lo these many years, that venerable chestnut about man's best friend—invented, I'm sure, by some sweet old gent with a weakness for the wet nose and the adoring gaze, and I'm all for it. But what people tend to forget when they become misty-eyed and the vapors overtake them is this: The arrangement between man and dog is partly practical. Friendship is all very well—if it weren't for friends, I wouldn't be here, after all—but one can't deny the importance of a warm bed, copious rations, and the run of a comfortable house.

One of my more gifted forebears must have realized this several thousand years ago and come to the conclusion that man was his most convenient support system. We dogs have our skills and talents, it's true, but can we guarantee a regular supply of food? No. Can we construct a snug and weatherproof shelter? No again. (Nor, for all their insufferable arrogance, can cats.)

And so the wise ancestor made the decision, in those primitive times long before the invention of kennel clubs and poodle parlors, to become a domestic accessory in a human household. Man, being highly susceptible to flattery, chose to take this as a pledge of friendship, brotherhood, true love, and all the rest of it, and so the myth was born. Ever since then, dogs have enjoyed flexible hours, trouble-free board and lodging, and, with a little luck and minimal effort, adulation.

That's the theory of it, at any rate, although my short experience up until then had been a little lacking in all respects, from kindly words to creature comforts. And now things had gone from bad to worse. I had a few apprehensive moments, sitting in solitary splendor up there in the hills, and there was even the odd thought about trying to find my way back to the devil I knew, boots and all. Fortunately, the sound of a car distracted me, and I made my way down the track to the road, hope springing eternal.

The car passed me by without slowing down. So did others in the course of the morning, despite amiable nods and leaps of greeting on my part. I experimented by sitting in the middle of the road, but they just drove around me, horns blowing and drivers showing a marked lack of sympathy. Such events put a strain on one's faith in human nature after a time. But finally, it occurred to me that my luck might change if I could catch people on foot. You can reason with people on foot, which you can't when they're rushing past at fifty miles an hour. There's no give-and-take with cars, if you know what I mean. And so I decided to find some pedestrians.

It was easier said than done, because my old hunting companion had chosen to drop me off in a spot that resembled what I've heard about New Zealand—trees, bushes, mountains, and very little else. A joy for those who like the unspoiled vista, I suppose, but not encouraging for the lonely traveler in search of company and succor. And so, with the wind in my face, I set off to see if I could find civilization.

The hours passed, and it must have been midafternoon when I first picked up a faint, familiar whiff of drains and diesel fumes. For you, perhaps, these have no particular significance and even less allure, but to me they spelled people. Sure enough, from the top of the next hill I could see a group of old stone

I set off to see if I could find civilization.

buildings, and as I came closer, I was able to make out
signs of activity, hustle and bustle and the sound of
voices. Not unlike ants, really, but noisier.

You must remember that my previous experience
of human habitations had been limited to the single
shabby ruin where I was born, and so this was a revelation to me—dozens of houses, and presumably hundreds of people. Somewhere among them, I felt sure,
was my future soul mate. It is delusions like this that
help you put one paw in front of the other at the end
of a hard day.

The village seemed enormous to me, streets leading off in all directions, strange and wonderful
aromas on every breeze, people strolling around in
that aimless way they do when they have nothing
much on their minds except what's for dinner. A
group of them had stopped to jabber at one another

on a corner, and this is where I learned a useful lesson in survival. People don't seem to be able to talk with their hands full. Don't ask me why, but when two or three of them get together to discuss the problems of the world, down go the bags and baskets on the ground, conveniently placed for those of my height to investigate. (My head would come somewhere between your knee and your waist, and comfortably over the top of any unattended basket.)

One shouldn't hesitate when opportunity knocks, and so I rescued a protruding baguette and retired with it to the shelter of a table outside the village café. I had just finished the final crumbs and was considering a return swoop on the basket when a hand came into view. It patted me on the head, disappeared, and came back holding a lump of sugar. I looked up to see a young couple at the next table beaming at me and making those faintly ridiculous sounds that humans always imagine speak volumes to the canine ear. They do the same with babies, too, I've noticed. But the tone of voice was welcoming, and a friendly hand is a pleasant change from a booted foot, and so I made myself agreeable.

Well, you'd have thought they'd never seen a dog before. More cooing, pats on the head, and sugar lumps coming down thick and fast, all the indications of love at first sight. Being a novice at the time, I took this as an invitation to follow them when they left the café, and I trotted along behind them, thinking—I won't deny it—that a soft bed and a new life were just around the corner. Call me naïve if you like, but since my experience of human behavior had been limited to abuse of one sort or another, I was unused to kindness and assumed more than I should have. Trouble often starts, I've now learned, when the friendly act is taken at face value. I had reason to believe, or so I thought, that my encounter with these young persons at the café was the beginning of a wonderful relationship. Alas, they didn't see it like that, and when we reached their car, there was a certain amount of embarrassed shuffling while I attempted to get in with them, ending with a firm shove outward and the door slamming a few inches north of my nose. There's a moral here somewhere about strangers bearing gifts, and I can be philosophical about it now, but it was a distinct setback at the time.

A lesser dog might have despaired. I've known spaniels, for instance, who have a tendency to collapse, roll over, and wave their legs in the air at the first hint of adversity. Not me. Resilience, that's the thing. Onward and upward. And so I decided to cheer myself up—as people frequently do, so I hear—by going shopping.

Working my way down the street, I was stopped in my tracks by the scent of heaven coming from an open doorway: fresh, raw meat—pork chops, legs of lamb, homemade sausage, tripe and liver, marrowbones, beef—and not a soul to be seen when I followed my nose inside. The drowsy hum of a tele-

I decided to cheer myself up by going shopping.

vision came from a room at the back, but apart from
that it was as quiet as the grave. I could even hear the
scuff of my paws on the sawdust-covered floor as
I made my way toward the profusion of delights
arranged on a scrubbed wooden table.

I thought I'd browse for a moment or two before
making my final selection, not realizing that the in-
decisive shopper often misses the best opportunities.
But I was limited to what I could carry in my mouth,
and I didn't want to snatch a piece of scrag end off
the table if there was a chance of steak. It's called the
exercise of informed choice. A fat lot of good it did
me, as events turned out.

A brace of pig's trotters had caught my eye, and
I was deliberating between them and a handsome
cut of veal when there was an almighty bellow from

the back of the shop. Enter the butcher, eyes
popping with fury as he looked around for reinforce-
ments. Luckily, the first weapon within reach was
a broom rather than a bone-saw or a cleaver, and
he wasn't too handy with that, knocking over a row
of glass jars—confit of duck, as I recall—in his eager-
ness to make contact with me. It helped to spoil
his aim, and I managed to jump over the debris and
make my departure with no more than a glancing
whack around the hindquarters. I should never have
dithered. He who hesitates stays hungry. I pass
this on as something to bear in mind when you're
shopping.

It was time to reconsider my tactics. If the episode
with the butcher was anything to go by, there was a
certain prejudice in the village shops toward dogs.
Remarkable, when you think of the instant havoc
that children can cause, and I've never known them
to be threatened with offensive weapons, but there
you are. One rule for some, and one rule for others.
And then it struck me as I watched a man and a mon-
grel leaving the bakery without being assaulted.
Maybe it wasn't all dogs that brought out the warlike
spirit; maybe it was just unaccompanied dogs. I went
up the street to the *épicerie* and waited outside to put
Plan B into action.

Like many great ideas, it was simple. I would
attach myself temporarily to a customer entering
the premises. Once inside, we would part company
to attend to our respective errands, and I would

leave, fully laden, while my personal shopper distracted the proprietor. It seemed to be foolproof.

There were some encouraging smells coming from inside the *épicerie*—not quite the range and red-blooded richness of the butcher's shop, but more than enough to set the imagination humming—and it was with a sharp sense of anticipation that I scanned the street for a likely accomplice.

I had never seen so many people before, and I think my lifelong interest in human behavior started on that late afternoon so long ago. All shapes, all ages, all sizes, jostling along together without any of the curiosity about one another that a group of dogs would display. No sniffing, no circling, no ceremonial leg lifting—very little of what I'd call social contact, apart from the occasional nod of the head or the clutching of hands. I'm used to it now, of course, but I remember thinking how strange it was, this lack of interest. Something to do with urban overcrowding, I shouldn't wonder. It must dull the senses.

I was so taken up with watching the passing parade that I jumped when I felt a woman's hand pat me on the head. Looking up, I saw an empty shopping basket and a smiling face, and then she'd gone, through the doorway and into the fragrant gloom of the *épicerie*. Seize the moment, I said to myself, and like a shadow I was there behind her, giving my best impersonation of an accompanied dog on official business.

It was a proper *épicerie,* of the traditional kind. So

many of them these days stock nothing more than cans and boxes and mysterious lumps wrapped in plastic, but here was real food, most of it naked— slabs of cheese, mountain sausage, cured hams, and a long row of cooked dishes. The French don't stint themselves, as you know, and there was everything from *crépinettes* of stuffed chicken to terrines that made my eyes water.

My companion stopped in front of the vegetables, which have never held any interest for me, and I slipped up the narrow aisle, disregarding the brief temptation of the biscuit section as I approached the back of the shop. This was where the treasures were displayed, and I was very taken by the homemade lasagne. But there was not a moment to be lost in contemplation. After my previous experience chez the butcher, I wasn't about to dawdle, and I was at full stretch on the hind legs, front paws on the counter and jaws about to close on a kilo of the best smoked ham, when all hell broke loose down below.

If you were feeling generous, you might have described the source of the problem as another dog— a spindly little object, knee-high to a rat, with an absurd, tightly curled tail that looked like a worm in torment and a piercing falsetto yap fit to wake the dead. For a moment, I thought he'd caught his personals in the ham slicer, but it was merely his miserable travesty of a bark. Hungry as I was, it was impossible to deal with the ham when he started to take flying bites out of my ankle, and it was while I was trying to shake him off that a mountain on legs, wearing a sour expression and an apron, appeared from the back to join in. I vaguely remember a rolling pin, too. All in all, it seemed unwise to linger.

So much for the welcome I received from the village shopkeepers, and all I can say is that you shouldn't trust those postcards of jolly natives simpering into the camera. The two I met that day would have given Genghis Khan nightmares. (They say he used to eat dogs, you know, when he ran short. I suppose we've made some progress since then.)

I returned to my previous refuge under the café table and reflected. One rejection and two attempts on my life in return for a small loaf of bread and a handful of sugar lumps. The afternoon had not been an outstanding triumph, and now the shadows were lengthening, evening was drawing nigh, and I was still no closer to bed and board than I had been when the day started. Tomorrow would bring new joys and opportunities, I felt sure, but in the meantime there was the problem of where to spend the night. To stay under the table or to seek shelter in the great unknown, that was the question.

It was answered by the café owner, armed with the ever-present broom that all villagers seemed to keep by their sides, presumably in case of invasion. He had come out to sweep the droppings of the day from under the tables and out into the street—for the general enjoyment of the public, I imagine. As he worked his way toward me, our eyes met. The broom was raised to the attack position. I would like to have contributed a small mark of appreciation for the warmth of his greeting, but there was no time for even a swift raising of the leg. Yet again, I left in haste, to seek peace in the countryside.

I was well clear of the village, musing on my latest taste of the milk of human kindness, when my nose was caught by a definite ripeness in the air. It was coming from the end of a narrow track, where a large bin had been overturned, its contents scattered on the grass. I came closer, nostrils twitching, and found that the problem of dinner had been solved. I studied the menu.

It never ceases to amaze me what people throw away. Bones, crusts, giblets, perfectly serviceable sardines—all these and more were set like jewels

The problem of dinner had been solved.

among the empty cans and paper and plastic. Pushing aside a discarded shoe, I was about to dust off the first course—a morsel of chicken skin *en gelée,* if memory serves—when I heard a growl. In fact, it was more like a snarl—unwelcoming rather than cheerful, anyway. I looked up to see the front half of a dog poking out of the bin, lips drawn back, teeth bared, hackles on red alert, the very picture of Fido defending hearth and home.

I like to think that I'm not without courage, particularly when the opposition is quite clearly old, infirm, and considerably smaller than me, all of which he was. And so I tried to ignore him while I finished off the chicken and moved on to some rather good cheese rind. But, as I'm sure you've found, it's not easy to enjoy your food when there's a constant and very tiresome whining going on a short distance from your ear. I've heard the same said about dinner parties that include investment bankers. You will know better than I, but apparently they have a compulsion to drone on. So it was with our friend in the bin.

However, apart from that small irritation, I did quite well for myself, thus sufficiently restored to consider the question of sleeping arrangements in a more hopeful light.

After a few minutes of exploration, a distinct pattern emerged. Leading off the village road, every few hundred yards on either side, were small tracks, each with a house at the end. And every track seemed

to have its own bin, similar to the one my peevish
dining companion had occupied. Applying the laws
of logic, I deduced that all of these bins would
contain an edible selection of one kind or another—
nothing to make the ears stand up, perhaps, but
enough to keep body and soul together, unguarded
and easily available. Sniffing confirmed my theory,
and I remember feeling quite gratified that brain and
nose were working as one for the greater good of the
stomach.

With tomorrow's breakfast taken care of, I turned
my attentions to the night's lodging, and here I
began to run into some unexpected obstacles. I must
have visited half a dozen houses, with a view to curling up for a few peaceful hours in an outbuilding, but
wherever I went, I was met by a volley of threats,
cries of alarm, and sounds of general disapproval—
not, in this case, from people, but from my own kind.
Every establishment had at least two resident dogs,
and from the fuss they were making, you'd have
thought I was trying to steal the family silver.

Fortunately, most of them were attached, by chain
or rope, to some immovable object. This hampered
their murderous instincts, and I was able to put them
in their place by marking their territory, leg raised
just out of range of their slavering jaws. That is considered an insult, you know, on a par with making
disparaging remarks about somebody's poor taste in
curtains, and I must say it drove them to a frenzy.
One of them—a big, mangy piece of work with outsize

teeth—threw himself against his chain so violently in his enthusiasm to get at me that he must have ruptured his vocal cords. His bark suddenly became a squeak, and he looked distinctly embarrassed. Served him right.

But these fleeting amusements weren't getting me any closer to a good night's rest. It had been a long, eventful, and instructive day, and I was tired enough not to be too particular about where I lay my head. As long as it was well away from brooms and jaws, it would do. I tried one last house, set off another hysterical symphony of howls and barking, and dug in for the night among the bushes at the edge of the forest.

The romantic notion of the forest, as I expect you know, is one of tranquil glades and leafy nooks, Mother Nature's haven of calm, a place for quiet repose. You should try living there, as I did over the next few weeks. My abiding memory of the forest is the noise. The screech of birds and their hideous dawn chorus first thing in the morning, hunters and their guns during the day, the endless rustling and slithering of nocturnal creatures, owls holding forth all through the night—the whole arrangement is my idea of bedlam. One tosses and turns, longing for unbroken slumber.

It reached the stage where I started to make regular visits to the village to get some relief from the din. As long as I maintained a prudent distance from the butcher and my other sparring partner in the *épicerie,* I had the run of the place and was left to loiter in peace. In fact, one or two of the less barbaric villagers began to recognize me and proffer the hand of friendship. But, as before, the hand was withdrawn as soon as I tried to convert it into something more permanent.

And then, when the vagabond's life was becoming less enjoyable by the day (and even less enjoyable by night), fate intervened. It was a milestone, or a turning point, or maybe even both. Anyway, I'll tell you what happened and you can judge for yourself.

I was on my way to the village after a night in the forest when the entire owl population seemed to have chosen my little corner as the place to have an argument. Or it might have been the mating season, although I'm not too sound on owls and their habits, so I couldn't say for sure. Whatever the reason, it was a shrill and sleepless night, and I was feeling very much the worse for wear as I walked along the road. Listless and wan, you might say, with hardly any of my customary bounce and esprit.

I heard a car behind me and hopped into the ditch to let it pass. But it stopped.

Out steps the lady driver, and I could tell at once she was a kindred spirit by one very simple act. Instead of peering at me from a great height, she crouched down so that our faces were more or less on the same level. It may seem like a small thing to you, but to a dog it indicates a great deal—sympathy, a desire to communicate on an equal basis, and, let's

not forget, plain good manners. Look at it this way:
If you were constantly being addressed by someone squinting down his nose at you from four feet
above your head, you wouldn't care for it. A lack of
common courtesy, you'd think, and you'd be quite
right. So you can understand why I responded to
madame's overtures with vigorous motions of the tail
and body, small cries of rapture, and a friendly paw
on her knee.

We stayed like this for several minutes, com-
muning by the side of the ditch, and then she seemed
to reach a decision. She opened the door of the car.
My ears drooped and my spirits fell, because previous experience had led me to recognize this as the
prelude to a hasty farewell, with the car going off into

My ears drooped and my spirits fell.

the sunset and yours truly left to carry on as before, the solitary wanderer.

But not this time. I was invited to get in, which I did, making myself as unobtrusive as possible on the floor. Imagine my surprise, not to mention the sudden rush of hope rekindled, when I was encouraged to sit on the seat next to my new best friend. We all have our ways of showing enthusiasm and excitement. Humans caper about and slap one another on the back when they feel it's called for; I prefer to chew something—not in an aggressive manner, you understand, but just to demonstrate approval of the current situation. And so I got to work on a convenient seat belt as we drove away from the village, back along the road, and turned up a track between two fields of vines.

It led to a house not unlike some of the others that I had visited during the past weeks, even down to the familiar sound of other dogs baying for my blood. There were two of them, and they weren't tied up, either, as I saw from the safety of the passenger seat. It took some coaxing from madame to get me out of the car and introduce me to the welcoming committee, but to my relief they were both bitches— a shaggy old biddy with a distant resemblance to a hunting dog and a black Labrador with a limp. They seemed harmless enough, and once the formalities were completed, they pottered off to collapse in the garden.

By this time, I was allowing myself to feel that there

might be more on the program of events than just a
visit. Madame had a thoughtful look in her eye as she
picked fragments of masticated seat belt from my
whiskers and took me indoors, murmuring something about the other member of the household. Let
it not be a cat, I remember thinking to myself, or a
homicidal case wearing boots and carrying a gun.
Funny how these thoughts flash through the mind
during decisive moments in one's life.

It turned out to be the other half of the management—unarmed and barefoot, which was a good
start, and looking slightly bemused. We exchanged
pleasantries, but I could sense that he didn't entirely
share madame's feelings, because they went off into
a corner for a tête-à-tête, leaving me to take a look at
my surroundings.

I'm no great judge of property from any point of
view but my own, but it appeared to be quite ade-
quate for my requirements—garden front and back,
the untamed wilderness a comfortable distance behind the house, rugs on the floor, and the scent of
the two bitches wherever one went. It was obvious
that they didn't sleep rough. All in all, it would do
me very well. And as there were two dogs in residence already, what difference would a third make?

I went across to where the management conference
was taking place and cocked an ear. There appeared
to be two issues under discussion, with madame
firmly on my side and the other half caught somewhere between pro and con. Were three dogs too

many? And if not, how and where would I fit in? There was a halfhearted argument put forward that my previous owner should be found, but madame knocked that one smartly on the head, letting fly in anguished style about ill-treatment, undernourishment, and lack of bedtime privileges. Then she moved on to more personal comments about my acne, protruding bones, and overall state of disrepair, ending with a plea on my behalf for intensive care and attention. It was music to my ears, and I moved over to lean against her leg as a gesture of solidarity.

She won in the end, bless her—wives usually do, I've noticed—and it was agreed that I would stay for a trial period. Well, I knew what that meant. If I kept my nose clean, deferred politely to the two bitches, and watched my step with the other half, I was in.

I remember as though it were yesterday rolling on the grass after my first decent meal for weeks, the management watching from the doorway, the sun on my belly and all well with the world. What a moment.

Night Maneuvers,
and a Confrontation
with Hygiene

*T*he rest of that day confirmed my first impressions, and it looked very much as though I had fallen on my feet. In the afternoon, we took a stroll along the path behind the house, and I began to change my views about the forest. It had certain merits if used for purely recreational purposes—an excellent selection of trees, small and terrified creatures scuttling off as one pounced on them, bosky and intriguing sounds in the undergrowth. I even came across the mature corpse of a pigeon, which I rolled in for several minutes, paying special attention to those hard-to-reach areas at the back of the neck and behind the ears. All in all, an amusing place to visit, the forest. I wouldn't want to live there, of course. And now I didn't have to.

We returned to the house, and there was more food. I wasn't used to such abundance, and after eat-

ing, it was all I could do to stagger under the table for
a siesta, using the well-upholstered Labrador as a pil-
low. By the time I woke up, darkness had fallen. Still
drowsy, I gradually became aware of whispered discussions between the management—complimenting
themselves, I hoped, on the good fortune that had
led me to their door.

In fact, the cocked ear then picked up a different
and rather ominous message. My sleeping arrangements were under review, and there seemed to be
a quite unnecessary concern about allowing me to
remain in the house. I think the lingering scent of
well-rotted pigeon around my neck and shoulders
may have come into it, and there was some mention
from the other half about leaving me free to return to
my previous address if I wanted to. I thought I'd
made it clear that I was quite content and not to be
disturbed under the table, but people can be remark-
ably insensitive at times, and I was hustled into the
night and taken to an outbuilding by the side of
the house.

I admit that it was an improvement over what I'd
been used to—thick blanket, bowl of water, bedtime
biscuit, pats of affection, and expressions of goodwill—but it wasn't indoors. And indoors was where I
wanted to be, head resting on a stout Labrador,
sleeping the sleep of one of the family.

But tonight, for some reason, wasn't the night, and
as the lights went out, I was left staring at the stars

through the open door of my modest chamber. I
mused, as one does at moments like this, on the
bewildering turns life can take—up one minute,
down the next, so near and yet so far, the rich tapestry of personal experience, and so forth. What would
Proust have done in similar circumstances? I wondered. Bawl for mother, I suppose, but then he
wouldn't have been in an outbuilding in the first
place. He was always indoors, as I remember.

I thought it worth trying one or two piteous howls,
complete with sobbing vibrato at the end, and waited
to see if the lights would go on. Sure enough, they
did, and out came the management, full of concern in
case I'd been savaged in my bed by a militant field
mouse. When they found me unscathed and ready to
accompany them back to the house, the mood of
sympathy changed. Stern words passed, and I was
told to settle down.

There are occasions when argument is fruitless—
I'm told that's the case when dealing with plumbers
and lawyers—and I sensed that this was one of them.
I heaved a sigh, and although my sighs are works of
art, long and wistful and infinitely touching, this one
had no effect at all. Two hearts of stone, wrapped in
their dressing gowns, left me to my solitary devices.
I was still wondering how I could convince them of
the error of their ways when I dozed off.

You know how it is sometimes when you sleep on a
problem? The subconscious gets to work, worrying

*Two hearts of stone, wrapped in their
dressing gowns*

away through the small hours, and in the morning,
voilà! The solution presents itself. That's exactly
what happened to me, because I awoke with a plan.

The mistake I had made, obviously, was in overes-
timating human intelligence. By and large, one cannot deny certain of mankind's achievements, such as
the invention of lamb chops and central heating, but
many people are strangely unreceptive to nuance.
The hint, the diplomatic nudge, the oblique statement—these very often pass straight over their
heads, and man and dog find themselves looking at
each other through a fog of incomprehension. Thus
it was with the management and myself. Delightful
and welcoming, they certainly were, but not, it

seemed, too quick on the uptake. Clearer signals were called for, but they needed to be executed with some delicacy. You can be too blunt sometimes, and it can end in tears, as a bullterrier of my acquaintance discovered when he started eating furniture because he felt unloved. No, finesse is the thing, and I think you'll agree that my scheme was a model of cunning and charm.

There was a pleasant, crisp feeling to the air as I emerged from my boudoir, with just enough breeze to carry an interesting variety of neighborhood aromas to the nose. I detected other dogs over to the east, mixed with the tantalizing smell of live chickens, and I made a mental note to pay them a visit as soon as domestic matters had been settled. The chicken, you see, is that happy combination of sport and nourishment. She runs and clucks in the most gratifying way when chased, and is also very tasty once the feathers have been dealt with. A useful bird, unlike most of them.

With plan firmly in place, I went up to the house. It was silent when I put my ear to the door, shutters closed, no hint of activity within. I had decided against barking in favor of less conventional methods, and I started scratching at the base of the door. It took a few minutes, but eventually I succeeded in rousing the two bitches—who should have been up and about anyway by this time, as it was well past dawn—and they raised their heads like a couple of second-rate sopranos and began to howl and carry on in fine style, which was exactly what I wanted. They would incur the full weight of disapproval for waking the household, and I would be sitting outside, lips sealed, good as gold and quiet as a stump.

It wasn't long before the door opened, and out rushed the two old girls in a state of high excitement, followed by the management, rubbing their eyes and blinking in the morning sun. Step one successfully completed. Once I was sure I had their full attention, I went back to the outbuilding, collected my blanket, and dragged it up to the door, wagging all the while. There, I thought to myself. If that doesn't indicate a sincere desire to cross the threshold, I don't know what will. But to be on the safe side, I shimmied over to madame, caught hold of her wrist gently in my jaws, and pulled her back into the house, making small and persuasive sounds as we went. I let go of her wrist, took up a sitting position under the table— back straight, paws together, head to one side, the docile and well-mannered hound—and awaited developments.

Both of them squatted down in front of me, and I gave them another short chorus of muted squeals. They were about to melt, I could tell, when I noticed madame wrinkling her nose, and then she used a word that meant nothing to me at the time: *toilettage.* Well, for all I knew in those days, it could have been an exotic breakfast cereal or the name of her mother-in-law, so I merely sat tight and tried to convey enthusiasm as best I could. In the light of subsequent

Night Maneuvers, and a Confrontation

I noticed madame wrinkling her nose.

experience, I might have been better advised to keep my distance until the persistent scent of dead pigeon had worn off, but we can all be wise after the event.

The important thing was that both blanket and I were permitted to stay in the house, and I took this to be a great step forward. I bustled helpfully about the kitchen with the rest of them while breakfast was being prepared and eaten, and I was of two minds as to staying under the table or risking a turn outside in the garden when I was summoned to the car. It appeared that the other half and I were going on an expedition.

We arrived at a village that I vaguely remembered from my travels and stopped outside a house that, even from a distance, had the noticeably strong and unappealing smell of disinfectant about it. This became worse as we went indoors, and I was instinctively getting into reverse to back out when I was gripped fore and aft by two meaty young women, taken into the chamber of horrors, and lifted bodily into a bath.

Traumatic is the only word to describe what happened next: drenched with water, smeared with soap, rinsed and soaped and rinsed again, and that was just the overture. There followed an interminable session with a miniature lawn mower, and then an attack by scissors, snipping away at ears, mustache, tail, and other sensitive regions. The final indignity was a dusting with powder that smelled like a mixture of Evening in Paris and weed killer.

Naked, perfumed, and highly embarrassed, I was at last delivered to the waiting room for collection. A poodle was there, I remember, looking down at me from the confines of her mistress's handbag and smirking in that way they do when they know they're safely out of range. You wait, I said to myself. By the time they've finished with you, there won't be anything left but a yap and four paws. I'm not too partial to poodles, as you can probably gather, but I did feel a twinge of sympathy for her.

So that was *toilettage,* and as far as I'm concerned, it ranks with kennels, obedience classes, rectal thermometers, and supervised celibacy as one of man's great mistakes.

But then, it was time for another surprise. I was driven back to the house and greeted as if I'd won the national lottery—biscuits, endless patting, cries of delight and admiration, photographs, the four-course hero's welcome, all of which I found rather puzzling. It had only been a shave and a shampoo, after all, even if it had been deeply unpleasant. Did these ecstatic demonstrations take place each morning after ablutions in the management's bathroom? I wouldn't rule it out. They have an odd liking for hygiene.

The morning's finale almost brought a tear to the eye. The other half went back to the car and returned to the house carrying a large circular basket, which he placed by the kitchen. Into the basket went my blanket, and that's when it dawned on me. The ghastly ordeal had not been in vain. It was my passport to the joys of indoors. I could take up my position as barker in chief, permanent resident, and defender of the premises against trespassing lizards and things that go bump in the night. No more subsistence living, no more boots in the ribs. A life of privilege—*luxe et volupté*—stretched before me.

It was a heady realization, and I thought of celebrating with a quick dive into the remains of the dead pigeon to get rid of the odor of cleanliness that clung to me, but I decided against it. If the management preferred the sanitary me, that's how I'd stay. Until tomorrow, at any rate. Pigeons always improve with age.

Name of a Dog

*E*xperience has taught me that christening a dog is by no means the straightforward business you might imagine it to be. Names last a lifetime, and terrible mistakes are made, usually with humorous intentions. I often think with sympathy of two acquaintances of mine, a pug called Gertrude Stein and Fang the Chihuahua. Very droll, no doubt, from the human viewpoint, but a daily embarrassment to the dogs concerned. It is no joke going through life as an object of ridicule. Fingers are pointed, and there is a great deal of vulgar mirth.

It's this warped sense of fun, you see, that carries some people away. Little do they realize the emotional scars they leave. It reached the stage with the long-suffering Fang where, after years of being giggled at, he became an almost total recluse. He took to spending the daylight hours under a bed, emerging only to answer calls of nature or to bite his owner on the lower reaches of the ankle.

Luckily, the management seemed to have some fairly sound views on names when trying to think of something suitable for me. I was lying in the courtyard on that fateful morning, having my stomach massaged by madame as the suggestions went back and forth, not taking a particularly active part in the proceedings myself, but interested enough to

An official title

stay awake. In my previous existence, I had been addressed only by grunts, blows, and curses, so the thought of having an official title was something of a novelty.

The question of length, for instance, had never occurred to me until I heard the other half putting forward the case for a single-syllable name. Easier for a dog's ear to pick up at a distance, he said, and easier for the human voice to cope with. Imagine having to shout Beauregard or Aristotle into the teeth of a howling gale. The lungs couldn't cope. And besides, he went on, long names become shortened in daily use, anyway. Remember Vercingetorix d'Avignon III, the prize beagle? They always called him Fred.

Madame was cooing away at me in that infinitely soothing fashion she has, telling me what a good boy I was, and I was responding with tail and upraised paw, when she paused in her ministrations and leaned down toward me.

"Boy?" she said. "Boy?"

Well, she clearly wasn't talking to the other half; it's common knowledge that his boyhood is a matter of distant history, and so I accelerated the tail and nodded at her politely, as one does when being spoken to. That seemed to do it.

"You see?" said madame. "He likes it. We'll call him Boy."

To be absolutely truthful, it was all one to me at the

time. I'd have answered to Heathcliff or Caesar Augustus or Mitterrand if it meant home cooking, civil treatment, and stomach massage, but they appeared to be pleased with the choice, and I've been Boy ever since. I'm obliged to them, really. It's honest, short, and serviceable. Rather like the better class of dachshund.

A Balanced
Education

I was a diamond in the rough in those early days, brimming with promise but somewhat deficient in the social graces. I'd never eaten from a bowl before. I had a cavalier attitude toward bodily functions, which caused one or two raised eyebrows with the management. I was unused to navigating around furniture. The world of gastronomy was unknown territory, and I was not at my ease with tradespeople. In other words, I lacked polish. Hardly surprising, really, when you consider that my first few months had been spent in solitary confinement, with occasional visits from a man whose idea of savoir faire was taking off his boots before going to bed.

However, I won't dwell on my humble origins, except to say that they had not prepared me for my new life of regular meals, sanitary habits, and harmo-

I had much to learn.

nious coexistence with two old bitches. I had much
to learn.

Fortunately, I was gifted, even then, with keen
powers of observation. There are those in this world
who merely look, but take nothing in; Irish setters
come to mind here, and I've heard the same said
about office receptionists, although I've never met
one. But I do more than look. I watch closely. I
absorb. I note and inwardly digest. I like to think of
myself as an eternal student of behavior—ants,
lizards, other dogs, people, they all fascinate me, and
studying their odd little quirks and rituals has
greatly helped my intellectual development, world-
liness, social composure, and all the rest of those
attributes one needs to live in harmony with man.

To start with, I paid particular attention to my
two roommates. These were the Labrador, in her
outfit of dusty black bombazine, and the senior

bitch, more rug than dog, who has been said by some people with highly suspect judgment to resemble me. The two of them, I assumed, had spent several years learning the ropes, and by using them as role models in matters of routine and general deportment, I would pick up the necessary domestic skills in no time, impress the management, and go to my natural place at the top of the class.

Have you ever tried living with two elderly females who are settled in their ways? Probably not, and if I were you, I wouldn't bother. They nag, you know, and tend to take offense at the most trivial things. I'll give you an example, which happened soon after I arrived, and which made me hobble for a week.

I told you I'd never eaten from a bowl. There's a knack to it, because if you're anxious to get at the rations, you tend to plunge in, and the more eager you are, the more the bowl skids away from you. I've since learned to jam it into a corner, where it can't escape, but at that time my technique was to place a paw in the bowl to keep it firmly anchored. I should also mention that I am not one of those fussy eaters who take an extended stroll between mouthfuls. I don't leave the bowl until it's empty, which I consider to be good sense and good manners, and I eat with gusto (some might say unfettered greed, but you have to remember my deprived upbringing).

In any case, I had finished and was sucking the last of it from my paw when I noticed that the bowl next to mine was unattended and half-full. I can't abide waste, and so I transferred the paw to the bowl next door and was about to deal with the contents when the senior bitch returned from her travels, found me tidying up what she'd left, and bit me extremely hard on the thigh. Snarls of outrage followed, and I was obliged to hop off smartly on three legs. So much for any sympathy I may have had for the feminist movement. They're more than capable of taking care of themselves, the gentle sex, and I have the scars to prove it.

But apart from their possessive attitude toward food, I found them to be reasonably good-natured and a great help in guiding me through the reefs and currents of daily domestic life. These are some of the lessons I learned:

It is permitted to bark at neighborhood dogs who have wandered off course, at the man who comes once a month trying to sell subscriptions to a yoga magazine, and at strangers at the gate. It is not permitted to bark at the telephone every time it rings, at the electrician on a mission of mercy, or at a centipede you find in your basket at three in the morning. Growling and dental displays are frowned on, as are major excavations in flower beds, the concealing of bones in visitors' handbags, and romps on the couch.

It is considered very bad form to break wind, and here I have to say that the Labrador excels. Unfortunately, once you make a name for yourself at this sort of thing, you tend to be treated with automatic suspicion, sometimes unfairly. I remember one winter evening, logs crackling merrily in the hearth, friends around the dinner table, we three dogs minding our own business as the banter flowed back and forth, when the atmosphere of well-being was sullied by a real torpedo, possibly the result of too much rich cheese. It was impossible to ignore, and conversation ceased while everyone looked for the guilty party.

Now I happened to be lying close to the perpetrator, a small and excitable man in journalism, as a matter of fact. But was there any attempt on his part to claim authorship? Certainly not. With the practiced effrontery that came, I'm sure, from many similar lapses in the past, he waved his wineglass in the direction of the Labrador and said, in so many words, Officer, arrest that dog. The poor old thing was expelled into the night, a victim of her reputation.

I wouldn't want you to think that my domestic education was limited to avoiding the disapproval of the management. Stemming, I suppose, from fondness and gratitude, and maybe a touch of self-interest, I also wanted to please them. It wasn't long before I picked up some invaluable hints on establishing myself in their good graces, laying up a store of benevolence against the day—accidents and misunderstandings will happen, as we all know—when it might be needed.

The human responds to spontaneous displays of affection. These can take the form of the straightfor-

*The human responds to spontaneous
displays of affection.*

ward, head-on-the-knee and adoring-gaze variety or
the early morning salute with tail at full wag, to more
complicated indications of joy, trust, fidelity, and a
desire to ingratiate. The transportation and delivery
of precious objects, for instance, never fails to please.
Following a trifling faux pas on my part, I once disin-
terred, with some reluctance, the remains of a mouse
that I had been saving until it reached full maturity
and placed it at madame's feet while she was in the
kitchen making mayonnaise. She was overcome with
gratitude; at least, I think it was gratitude. She summoned the other half, and they both regarded the
mouse with expressions of wonder. Rather touching,
really, and well worth the minimal effort involved,
since I was forgiven immediately. I've had much the
same gratifying reaction to other tokens of esteem—
cushions, hats, mislaid airline tickets and discarded

A Balanced Education

items of lingerie from the guest quarters, a favorite book, urgent faxes from foreign parts, or the back half of a grass snake. The nature of the gift doesn't seem to matter. It's the fact that I take the trouble to choose it personally that counts.

I'm a quick study when there's some advantage in it for me, and so it wasn't long before I mastered the routine of everyday domestic life and could turn my attentions to learning about the outside world. Here, of course, I had to rely more on the management, and it is probably appropriate at this point to give you a brief character sketch.

They are not like other couples, I've discovered, in that both of them stay at home. In normal circumstances, so I hear, people leave the house in a bad temper shortly after breakfast and go to work. They have offices where important and serious activities take place, meetings and paperwork and what have you. This is not the case *chez nous*. Honest employment is avoided, and I sometimes wonder why. Madame seems perfectly capable, particularly in the kitchen, and I would have thought that a steady job in a canteen would not be beyond her.

The other half, alas, is not visibly gifted. I have observed his attempts at gardening and minor domestic tasks over the years, and they usually end in pain or bloodshed: Wounds from screwdrivers, shovels, and pruning shears; scalded fingers from kitchen utensils; broken toes caused by clumsiness with heavy objects; and temporary blindness from a

71

poorly aimed salvo with the rose spray are only some of his disasters. Thank heaven he doesn't hunt. He is not dexterous, except for a certain facility with the corkscrew. Even this small skill could be put to commercial use—bars need bartenders, after all—but he shows no signs of ambition, preferring to shut himself in a room for extended periods, sharpen pencils, and gaze at the wall. Odd, if you ask me.

Nevertheless, they appear to be contented enough, and the arrangement suits me very well. It's not often, as I'm sure you've found out, that you like both members of a couple, and here I consider myself fortunate—happy with either, happier with both. They're punctual with the food, great believers in the benefits of fresh air and exercise, and solicitous over my ailments. They place rather too much emphasis on hygiene for my liking, but nobody's perfect, and in terms of general care and attention, I don't have any serious complaints. If I'm allowed one criticism—and as this is my book, I think I am—it is simply that they are unable to come to terms with their own social habits, which can be a little exasperating from time to time.

They claim, loudly and often, to be lovers of the quiet life, content to vegetate, admire the beauties of the countryside, and tuck themselves up with the bedtime cocoa shortly after the sun's golden orb sinks slowly in the west (their words, not mine). This is self-deluding nonsense. For two people who like to believe they're one step removed from the hermit of the woods, they're dismal failures. I can't remember the last time we had a day when the house was empty. If it's not neighbors or the men who seem to be on permanent duty with a cement mixer, it's a deputation of refugees from overseas—a boisterous, disreputable collection, by and large, addicted to drink, late hours, loud music, and gossip.

Not that I mind. It's rarely dull, and if, like me, you have a healthy curiosity about the ways of the world, there's no place quite as illuminating as my spot under the dining table, learning by eavesdropping.

This has been going on for years now and has provided me with what you might call a wide-ranging, eclectic education. I know, for instance, that 1985 was a particularly good vintage in Châteauneuf; that one of the local mayors likes dressing up in a nurse's uniform and playing the trumpet; that all politicians and lawyers are rogues; that writers are saintly and hard-done-by artists, exploited by brutal publishers; that the Channel Tunnel will be the end of England as we know it; that a baker in the next village has eloped with an exotic dancer from Marseille; that a diet of foie gras and red wine prolongs life expectancy; that the European Economic Community is run by venal buffoons; that the British royal family is moving to Hollywood; and so it goes on. All human life is there, and it's fascinating stuff if you can stay awake.

What is sometimes even more interesting is the

critical assessment that is delivered in the kitchen once the revelers have left, and here we return to the management.

I try never to miss these gentle exchanges as the empty bottles are counted and the dishes are being dropped, and there's a comforting familiarity about the course the conversation takes. It starts with a brisk difference of opinion about the quality of the food, with madame expressing disappointment with her cooking, and the other half pointing to the evidence of bare plates and bones picked clean.

This is followed by a prolonged discussion of the highlights of the evening's entertainment and personal remarks, which we needn't go into here, about the various guests. Act three is a unanimous vote to avoid all social contact for the next six months. But then we have the encore, which is the realization that invitations have been accepted for a replay. And so to bed. You see what I mean? They say one thing ("Never again"), then do precisely the opposite ("See you next Tuesday").

But the constant flow of guests has been instructive, as I hope you'll see from the pages that follow, and by keeping eyes and ears open, I gradually learned much of what I know today. You could say that observation and eavesdropping have provided me with a sound intellectual base. For practical knowledge, however, there is no substitute for experience in the school of hard knocks. I give you the incident of the plumber under the sink.

A Balanced Education

Henri is his name, and he appears frequently at the house toward the end of the morning to arrange his tools on the kitchen floor. This is an apparently vital part of the plumbing process, a kind of limbering up before the mysteries of valve, spigot, and overflow are investigated. And so he lays out his rows of hammers, adjustable wrenches, drills, blowtorches, and his special hat with the lamp on the front for peering into dark corners, looks at his watch, and goes off to lunch. The master plumber, so he says, cannot plumb on an empty stomach. Madame is left to pick her way through the equipment and mutter, in her usual way, about giving it all up and going to live in a tent, and the other half, in his usual way, finds something pressing to do as far from the kitchen as possible.

Normally, I don't pay too much attention to plumbing, but on this occasion I was intrigued. For some days, there had been an interesting and increasingly strong aroma coming from the closet under the sink. I couldn't place it myself, but I overheard Henri saying that, in his professional opinion, there was a small, dead creature, or maybe even a nest of them, lodged somewhere in the pipes. I'm never averse to a corpse, as long as it's not mine, and so I decided to supervise activities and see for myself exactly who was hiding in the kitchen's intestinal tract.

Henri returned from lunch and the management went into hiding, a habit of theirs in the face of potential catastrophe. Ever since the unfortunate business with the upstairs ball cock, I think they fear the worst whenever Henri pits himself against the plumbing, and I must admit he has a patchy record: played thirty-two, won ten, and lost the rest, and that was just since I'd been keeping score. Anyway, with the management well out of harm's way, there were just the two of us in the kitchen.

Henri adjusted his hat and switched it on, crawled on all fours under the sink, and started the process of diagnosis, which was to hit everything in sight with a hammer. He talks to himself while he's working, and so I was more or less able to keep track of progress, although there wasn't much in the way of excitement, unless you have an interest in corroded joints and deformed waste pipes.

And then he must have found what he was looking for, because there was a sudden intake of breath, and *voilà!* was mentioned a couple of times in a satisfied way before he reversed out of the closet to rummage through his collection of instruments on the floor. I took his place under the sink, and it was immediately obvious to me where the foreign body was, halfway up the U-bend. I was amazed he couldn't smell it himself, but that's plumbers for you, I suppose— all brute force and wrenches, and very little talent in the nostrils.

It was a vole in there, I was fairly certain, and I was thinking of somewhere suitable to bury it when there was a tap on my back, and I turned around to see

A Balanced Education

Henri and his illuminated hat. He was anxious for me to leave, I think, because he dragged me out by my back legs, called me something insulting, although technically accurate, and shoved me aside on his way into the closet.

Something in the genes took over then, a wild, primitive desire to be in at the kill. Also, it was as much my closet as his. I squeezed back in so that I could look over his shoulder and witness the extraction of the vole at close quarters. Henri elbowed me out. I pushed my way in again. And so it went on for several minutes. It was a battle of wills, but eventually my determination prevailed, as it usually does. Dogs are more single-minded than people, you see, as you'll know if you've ever watched anyone trying to coax a Jack Russell out of a rabbit hole.

I think Henri would have shrugged if there had been room, but he nodded at me instead, beckoned me to come closer, and went to work with an adjustable wrench. Simple, trusting soul that I was, I thought our territorial differences had been resolved, so I put my chin on his shoulder, the better to see what happened next. A mistake. He performed one last turn with the wrench, ducked aside, and let me have the full benefit of the dead vole and several gallons of pent-up water right between the eyes. He blamed me for the subsequent flooding, too. Moral: Never trust a plumber in a confined space.

It's the kind of experience that leaves an emotional mark, and I'm sorry to say that there have been

others. Take the postman, for instance, who objects
to my running out for a harmless frolic with his van
and keeps a handful of gravel at the ready to throw at
me. Or the cyclist who tried to part my hair with his
pump; he lost his balance and fell off, as it happened,
and retired hurt, with torn shorts and blood pouring
down his leg. That was a just and satisfactory ending, but there have been times when things haven't
worked out quite the way they should have—the
chicken-training episode, for one. I'll deal with that
later, but I think you take my point. Pitfalls abound,
and people are unpredictable. The world can be a
perilous place.

The Art of
Communication

I am, so I've been told, an ornament to any household, an amiable companion, a patient listener, a sage, a source of continuous entertainment, and a mobile burglar alarm. But I have discovered over the years that these virtues are not enough for some people. They are almost always female, in my experience, and they share several characteristics, all resulting, I suspect, from being exposed to too many fairy stories when young. There is no better example of the breed than one of our local landmarks, Madame Bilboquet, a large lady of a certain age who is devoted to good works and vintage port, which she considers to be *très anglais*.

She wears billowy clothing in pastel colors and smells of dried flowers that have been kept a little too long in a drawer. Her handbag tastes of talcum powder. She collects porcelain figurines of stout pigs

and ruminant cows. She writes letters on paper that
has bunny rabbits skipping along the bottom. You
know the sort. Her heart's in the right place, no
doubt, but she has this unfortunate tendency to
gush.

I can tell what's coming when she fixes me with
a moist and sentimental eye and smiles. If I don't
take evasive action, she will pat the top of my head in
that dainty, hesitant way people adopt when they
pick up a dead sparrow. Then she sighs. And it
starts. "Isn't he sweet?" she says, in the voice she
usually reserves for her wretched rabbits. "I wonder
what he's thinking."

Most of the time, it's about sex, or where the next
meal's coming from, but of course she's not to know
that. I'm tempted to put an end to the matter by
plunging into a noisy investigation of my undercar-
riage. But I don't. I humor her. One never knows
with Madame Bilboquet. She has been known to keep
biscuits in what she calls her reticule. So I adopt my
most soulful expression and brace myself for the
inevitable.

Sure enough, after another gusty sigh, out it
comes, the missing ingredient. "Don't you wish he
could talk?"

I ask you. There she is, a grown woman, spouting
drivel that would embarrass a poodle, and we all
know what little toadies *they* are. The fact is, I have no
need to talk. I can make my feelings and wishes perfectly clear to anyone who has the most rudimentary

powers of observation. The management understands me. The neighbors understand me. We had one of the local tax inspectors around here the other day. He's no Einstein, but even he seemed to understand me. He left in a hurry, actually, with one leg of his trousers slightly damp, but that's another story.

Anyway, I may not talk, but I like to think that I am one of the great communicators. I have a manly and distinctive bark, an eloquent sniff, a squeal of horror that serves to discourage any attempts at grooming. I have, so I'm told, a most expressive snore. And my growl is a model of menace, a profundo rumble that strikes terror into the hearts of small birds and hesitant salesmen. Unfortunately, it gives me a sore throat, so I use it sparingly.

You will have noticed that these abilities, while impressive in their octave range and variety, are all based on sound. And, let's be honest, most dogs can make a noise when it suits them, although perhaps not always with perfect timing and sense of pitch. Noise, in any case, is not always the way to get what you want. Ask any politician. He'll tell you that well-directed flattery and, if you have a strong stomach, the occasional bout of baby kissing will produce more satisfactory results than shouting. So it is with dogs and people. Charm succeeds where yapping fails. Take it from me.

The key to it all, in my opinion, is what sociologists call "body language." The supplicant paw, the vibrating tail, the fixed and loving gaze, the shudders of rapture—these speak louder than words when used by an expert. And I like to think that I'm an expert; heaven knows, I've had plenty of practice.

Let me give you an example, which happened only the other day. It had rained all morning, and the management had decided to go out and have a long lunch. This is frequently their reaction to unpleasant weather. Inconsiderate of them, I know, but there it is. And so I was left in the house with the other dogs—dear old souls in many ways, but somewhat lacking in pioneer spirit. Reluctant to join in, if you know what I mean. I think they probably suffered from too much training during their formative years and never recovered.

As I always do when cooped up and left to my own devices, I made a tour of the premises—checking the kitchen for any edible traces of sloppy housekeeping, testing doors and electrical wiring, rearranging rugs, and generally making myself useful. And then, on a whim, I decided to have a look upstairs, where overnight visitors are locked up. For some reason, this has been designated a forbidden zone. Heaven knows what they do up there, but it's been made clear to me that I'm not welcome.

So up the stairs I went, and what did I find? The door had been left ajar, and the delights of what is grandly referred to as the "guest suite" were available for inspection.

Well, once you've seen one bathroom, you've

seen them all. Stark, uncomfortable places that reek of soap and cleanliness. But the bedroom was a different matter altogether—wall-to-wall carpet, cushions galore, a large bed. And rather a fine bed at that—not too high, with an ample supply of pillows and an inviting expanse of what I later found out was an antique bedspread. It looked like the standard-issue white sheet to me, but antique linen isn't one of my interests. I incline more to the fur-rug school of interior decoration myself.

Nevertheless, the bed had a definite appeal—as it would to you if you normally spent your nights in a basket on the floor—and so I hopped up.

At first, I was a little disconcerted by the degree of softness underfoot, which reminded me of the times when I'd accidentally trodden on the Labrador. But once I adapted my movements, I found I could explore in short and rather exhilarating bounces, and I made my way up to the head of the bed, where the pillows were kept.

They were poorly organized, in my view, laid out in a neat row, which may suit the reclining human figure but is not a convenient arrangement for a dog. We like to be surrounded when we sleep. I think it may be a subconscious desire to return to the womb, although I personally wouldn't want a second visit. As you may remember, I had to share with twelve others, and I have no pleasant memories of the experience. Even so, the instinct to surround oneself remains, possibly for protection, and I set to work dragging the pillows to the middle of the bed, until they formed a kind of circular nest. And there I settled, in great comfort, and dozed off.

Sometime later, I was wakened by the sound of a car and the barking of the two old bitches downstairs. The management had obviously gorged enough and had decided to return.

You may not know this, but people who live with dogs like a full turnout when they come home after an absence. It makes them feel loved and appreciated. It can also make them feel slightly guilty at having left their faithful companions all alone. This, in turn, can lead to what they call "treats" and what I regard as conscience payments to make up for willful neglect. However you look at it, the fact is that it's usually worth presenting yourself at the door with bright eye and jaunty tail and generally behaving as if life had been an arid desert without them. As it happens, I could happily have spent the rest of the afternoon on the bed, but I bounded downstairs to do my duty and lined up with the others as the management made their entrance.

All was well until that evening, when madame went up to put some flowers and a decanter of insect repellent in the guest room for visitors who were arriving the next day. She is fastidious about these little touches and has been known to agonize over such details as the choice of water—fizzy or flat—to leave on the bedside tables. She wants guests to be comfortable, you see, which I feel only encourages them to stay. The other half, in contrast, is all for giving them the earliest possible au revoir, which just goes to show that marriage can be a question of give-and-take. Anyway, there was madame upstairs in the honeymoon suite.

I heard distant cries of alarm, put two and two together, and assumed that my adjustments to the bedding were causing some minor distress. Consequently, I was in the basket faster than a rat up a drainpipe and feigning the sleep of the innocent by the time she came down. There were three of us, I reasoned, and so there was a fair chance that one of the bitches would be sentenced to bread and water while the true culprit escaped. Wrongful arrest and imprisonment is very popular these days, so I've heard, and I was hoping that this would be another chapter in the annals of injustice.

With eyes tightly shut and ears tuned in to the hurricane warning, I listened to madame as she waxed indignant about footprints on the bedspread, ripped and rumpled pillows, and one or two other small imperfections that were going to disqualify us from winning House of the Year award.

I heard her coming over to my basket, and I ventured a half-open eye. Madame's accusing figure stood before me, brandishing the evidence, shaking the offending bedspread in front of me and carrying on as though I'd thrown up in her best hat (which I did once, but there were extenuating circumstances). I attempted the nonchalant and puzzled

reaction, but what I'd failed to take into account was
the size of my paws and the traces of mud that
remained on them after the morning walk. Taking
hold of one incriminating paw, she applied it to a
large and well-defined footprint, and that was that.
Dead to rights, guilty as charged, and serious reper-
cussions on the way, I felt sure—unless I moved
quickly.

One lesson I've learned in life is that everything is
negotiable. No crime, however foul, is beyond re-
demption. You can steal the Sunday lunch, shred
books, bite off the heads of live chickens, and pretty
much despoil to your heart's content as long as your
conciliation technique is sound. It's known as plea
bargaining, and it has allowed far worse villains than
I to walk away unpunished, with scarcely a blot on
their escutcheon. If you don't believe me, read the
newspapers.

Punishment in our house, as in the legal system
generally, depends not only on the gravity of the
offense but also—and this is possibly more important—on the mood and general disposition of the
presiding judge and the jury. There are days when a
petty misdemeanor can lead to physical retribution
and temporary exile; on other occasions, all you get
for the same infringement is a verbal warning and
half an hour's probation, with remission for good
behavior. A tricky thing, justice. You can never tell
which way it's going to jump.

The atmosphere on this particular evening was

Punishment in our house

fraught. I suspect it was not merely the nature of the crime but also the effects of an excessive lunch, which often come to the surface in the early part of the evening: nagging headache, dyspepsia, and bloat, accompanied by short temper. The judge was going to go for the maximum sentence, in my estimation, and so I decided to hold nothing back. The full repertoire was called for. It was time for some advanced body dynamics, or what I prefer to call the "seven gestures of appeasement." I pass them on to you in the hope that you never need to use them.

One

Roll over on the back, after the fashion of the cocker spaniel, and wave the legs helplessly. This serves to indicate remorse and to foil the first instinct of the angry human, which is to administer painful blows to the hindquarters. You cannot smack them at floor level with any degree of force.

Two

The tone of voice will tell you when the heat of the moment has subsided and it's safe to get up and approach the judge and jury. This should be done with the modified shimmy—head down in shame, with the rest of the body wriggling in a frenzy of apology. Soft, contrite sounds are appropriate here if you have the knack of making them. Avoid barking or any baring of the teeth.

Three

Sit. Raise the right paw and place on the nearest available knee. For some reason, most people consider this endearing, and the chances of a clip around the ear are remote.

Four

Remove the paw and rest the full weight of the head on the chosen knee. In most cases, this will provoke an involuntary pat, and then you know you're home and dry. If it doesn't work, proceed with the rest of the program.

<u>Five</u>

Establish the whereabouts of a hand. After making sure that it isn't holding a glass of red wine, butt it with a firm upward motion of the head. I mention the red wine only because of an unfortunate accident that I was once blamed for, quite unfairly, which rather spoiled the magic of the moment.

<u>Six</u>

By now, all should be forgiven, but it's important to be seen not to celebrate too quickly. I always take the time for a few tender minutes of affectionate leaning—against a leg or an arm, whichever is most convenient. The appendage doesn't matter; it's the endearing gesture that is vital.

And that, nine times out of ten, should do the trick. Only in desperate situations, when every blandishment has met with grim rebuff and hideous threats persist, do I have to resort to the ultimate solution and unleash my secret weapon.

I should explain the history of it. Some years ago, one of my admirers presented me with a life-size replica of the traditional Christmas cracker in bright red rubber, with festive green sprigs of rubber holly at either end, a definite collector's piece. It happens to be a very satisfying object to hold in the mouth;

well-shaped and with just the right amount of give. You've probably never held the upper part of a squirrel's back leg between your teeth. I have, and my cracker has a similar consistency. Firm but yielding, if you follow me. The other similarity to the squirrel is that my cracker squeaks when bitten. This amuses me, and for reasons that I couldn't begin to explain, it makes people laugh. Never fails. And so, in extremis, when catastrophe looms, do I give up and wait for my just deserts? Do I cower under the withering gaze of disapproval? Certainly not. I fetch my cracker.

Seven

Even here, a certain delicacy of touch is necessary. Constant squeaking irritates the human ear, as I've noticed many times when the television is on, and so I sit with cracker clenched between the teeth, looking as forlorn as possible, and squeak at irregular intervals. And, what do you know, it always works. Always. Heaven knows why, but within seconds the storm clouds disappear and I am restored to grace, thanks to the squeak that turns away wrath. There's a lesson here somewhere for mankind, and if you ever find yourself involved in litigation, my advice is to make sure you have a rubber cracker in your pocket.

Mano a Mano
with the Cat
in the Garage

The world, as Jean-Paul Sartre might have said had the thought occurred to him, is divided into those who like cats and those who don't. I'm a founding member of the second group, which will come as no surprise to you when I tell you how cats and I first became acquainted. It was during my infancy, when, as I've mentioned, times were hard and food was scarce—for us dogs, at any rate. It was a different bag of bones for the house cat.

Hepzibah by name, malignant by nature, she spent her days dozing indoors and, from the look of her, was grossly overfed. She was bigger than we were then—a monstrous, beady-eyed creature covered in mottled black and brown fur, with one long yellow tooth protruding over her bottom lip and a full set of claws, which all of us puppies felt at one time or another. Every evening at feeding time, she would

waddle down and join us in the barn to inspect the
chef's offerings—knowing that, by mistake probably,
we were occasionally given something more appetiz-
ing than stale bread and gristle. Whenever that happened, Hepzibah would lay about, cuffing us right
and left to get to the trough first. And, do you know,
it must have been for sport. It couldn't have been
from hunger; she was built like a sofa.

To this day, after that youthful trauma, I can never
look on cats with any genuine enthusiasm, and I
never cease to marvel at the popularity enjoyed by
Felis domesticus. What is he, after all, but an anti-
social fur ball with delusions of superiority?

The rot started thousands of years ago, as any
historian will tell you, with the Egyptians. For some
reason—addled brains due to the climate, possibly,
or madness brought on by building too many pyra-
mids—they elevated the status of the cat from common mouse catcher to religious object, protector of
the Pharaoh's Kitty Litter and icon in chief. Cats,
of course, being altogether too pleased with themselves from birth onward, took this as their due
and lorded it over the desert sands, taking a front
seat at King Tut's dinner parties, having their paws
anointed with sacred unguents, giving up mousing
for a life of idleness, and generally being obnoxious.
And that has been their lot ever since.

When the rule of the Pharaohs collapsed—which it
was bound to do, given the misguided people in

charge—you might have thought that the world would have learned a simple lesson in cause and effect: Namely, cat worshipers come to a sticky end. The best they can hope for is a full-length bandage and parking space in a badly ventilated tomb. And another thing: You won't find Tiddles curled up at their feet in eternal loyalty. If he's given half a chance, he's off looking for the next soft touch.

Well, you may say, those were dark and primitive days, and we've come a long way since. Knowledge has increased in quantum leaps, and now we have more modern gods—television, for instance, or football players. If that is your opinion, dear reader, I must tell you that the cat movement has not only survived but prospered mightily, its furry tentacles reaching everywhere one looks.

Take the arts. There are paintings of cats, volumes of prose and poetry devoted to cats, racks of ghastly greeting cards with Pussy smiling his supercilious smile. There is even, so I hear, a cat musical. I'd quite like to see that, actually, because the thought of grown men and women prancing around in false tails and nylon whiskers appeals to my sense of the absurd. I dare say the show is a sellout in Egypt.

All this—and there's much more, but I won't belabor the point—is by way of explaining my position vis-à-vis the cat. I am not a fan. Call it sour grapes if you like, or blame it on the horrendous Hepzibah, but when I think of those overstuffed creatures hav-

ing the run of the furniture and creamed-chicken
gourmet dinners, it makes the blood boil and gives
me grave doubts about mankind's sense of priorities.

Ours is an enlightened household, I'm happy to
say, and so, apart from the occasional sighting of cats
slinking through the forest on some furtive errand,
I'm not bothered by them. I certainly don't expect to
find them anywhere on my rolling acres, and least of
all in the garage. But one morning not long ago, I was
strolling past the open garage door on my way to do
some light work among the lizard population, when I
was stopped short by my nose. There it was, strong
and unmistakable: the scent of cat.

There's a popular misconception—shamelessly
encouraged, of course, by ostentatious displays of
washing and licking and paws behind the ears—that
the cat is one of nature's cleaner creations, odor-free
and community-minded when it comes to waste dis-
posal. This is bunk. Put a ripe old tomcat in an en-
closed space, such as the garage, and you'll need to
hold your breath. It's that bad.

I put my head inside the door and looked around.
To help you set the scene in your mind's eye, I
should tell you that the garage would not win any
prizes for neatness and order. The car sits in the
middle, surrounded by sacks of fertilizer, lengths of
garden hose, a lawn mower, three or four garden
chairs resting between engagements, drums of rose
spray, old clay pots, and a range of shelves that hold
everything from cans of paint to a chain saw. For all

their talents, I never suspected the management of larceny, but this muddle of equipment looks as though it had been removed under cover of night from a hardware store and tossed willy-nilly into its new home as it came off the back of the truck. And somewhere, hiding among the wreckage, was the trespasser.

Through the door I went, moving with infinite menace, and looked around. Nothing stirred. He was probably pressed up against the wall, frozen with terror, or maybe he'd tucked himself behind the potting soil, but he wasn't in any of the obvious places. They like to hide under cars, you know, which is why you often see them with an elegant smear of car oil down their backs. This one, however, had gone into deep cover.

I knew he was there, though, by the smell, and so I picked my way through the clutter toward the shelves at the back, the nose questing and every sense on the qui vive, a lethal weapon poised to strike. And then I saw him—or, to be strictly accurate, part of him.

The highest shelf was used for the storage of shallow wooden seed trays, stacked in a pile, and I noticed that the topmost tray seemed to have grown a tail. A bushy, ginger, grubby-looking thing it was, similar to the brushes people use to clear a blocked drain, and, in my view, equally unsavory. It was hanging over the side of the tray. Aha, I said to myself. Follow the tail and you find the cat.

I noticed that the topmost tray seemed to have grown a tail.

The plan was to give the dangling tail a sudden yank and see if our ginger visitor could break the world record for unassisted flight by getting out of the garage without touching the ground. But much to my irritation, the end was just out of reach, even at full stretch on my hind legs. I was pacing back and forth, mulling over tactics and determined to preserve the element of surprise, when I felt that I was being watched. It's a knack I have, a kind of extrasensory perception developed during the old days of living rough and dodging brooms, and it hasn't failed me yet.

I looked up, and there was a sight to curdle the cream. Pussy's head had appeared, the size of a small melon, with two badly mangled ears and eyes the color of old rabbit droppings. I'm a generous soul, so I'll merely say he wouldn't have won any beauty contests and leave it at that. We looked at each other in silence for a few seconds, and then I decided to show him that I had no intention of taking in lodgers. Up on my hind legs I went, and I gave him the full treatment. I snarled; I barked; I foamed at the mouth with blood lust. You can't imagine the savagery of it all unless you've been to a literary cocktail party with no restrictions on the drink. And do you know what he did? He yawned, closed his eyes, and gave every appearance of going to sleep.

I was getting a little hoarse by this time and, to be honest, not too sure of my next step, when there was a sudden gust of wind, and the garage door slammed shut like an explosion. That woke the brute up, and he was out of the seed tray and standing at attention behind the lawn mower in a split second.

He was, if it's possible, even less prepossessing at ground level, and it was made worse by the ridiculous attitude he'd assumed. His tail was pointing to the sky, his back was arched, his fur stood straight up, as if he'd just swallowed some high-voltage milk, and his tattered ears were pressed flat against his moth-eaten head. I remember thinking he'd be out of luck if he auditioned for the musical, and then events moved rather quickly.

We sparred for a few seconds, with me bobbing and weaving and him taking a few unsuccessful swipes with his paw before he realized he was outclassed. I had him on the run. Through the paint pots and empty bottles we went, scattering all before us until we came to the door, which, as I've told you, was shut. Now I had him where I wanted him. Pause for breath before round two.

This was when I learned another piece of practical wisdom, which I urge you to bear in mind should circumstances require. The cornered opponent with nowhere to go is not to be trusted. They say that about rats, as you know, and highly placed government officials who are caught with their hands in the till or their trousers down, and it's quite true. They lash out, ignoring the possible consequences, causing pain and woe to innocent parties—which is exactly what happened to me.

I had the intruder with his back to the ropes, in a manner of speaking, up against the garage door, with no chance of escape. Had he surrendered peacefully, I would just have given him a swift mauling and sent him on his way, but he came out of the corner like a thing possessed and caught me one on the muzzle, with a surprising amount of force for a small, tubby creature. He had all his claws out, too. Instinct must have taken over then, I suppose, because the next thing I knew, I'd taken a flying leap backward and upward, landing on the hood of the car. Undignified, you may think, but then you weren't on the receiving end.

It was at this point that the management, attracted by the noise of our negotiations, came to the cat's rescue by opening the door. He went off like a flea on skates, with me in moderately hot pursuit, and found refuge in the high branches of an almond tree. I took up a position at the base of the tree, growling and stamping and flexing my whiskers as though I was spoiling for action, but if truth be known, I was quite happy to leave things as they were. But it was not to be.

One of the disadvantages of country life is that you are never completely free from the curiosity of your neighbors, who will take every opportunity to stop what they're doing to watch what *you're* doing. I was on my hind legs, giving a convincing impression of trying to climb the tree, when there was a shout from the vineyard below the house.

"Attention!" said the voice, "that is the cat of Madame Noiret! He is old and delicate! Disengage your dog!"

We looked around, the management, the cat, and I, to see a ragged figure sitting on his tractor, flapping his arms in a frenzy, as the French tend to do in moments of crisis. I barked. The cat hissed and moved up a couple of branches. The other half seized me from behind. The busybody dismounted from his tractor and stumped up the drive to join us.

He insisted on shaking hands, which gave me the chance to slip out of the other half's clutches and put some distance between us. I declined the management's invitation to get back in the house, and I sat out of reach, waiting for gravity to work its magic on the cat. He was by now perched uneasily at the very top of the tree, swaying in the wind, and I had pleas-

ant visions of his bough breaking—the almond is not
all that sturdy—and the ginger missile plummeting
to earth. Thus perish all trespassers.

Alarm and consternation at the base of the tree.
The cat must be rescued; Madame Noiret must be informed. A *crise dramatique*—what are we to do? I
knew what I was going to do, which was to evade
arrest and wait for the intruder to fall off his perch.
It looked increasingly likely as the wind freshened,
and I was interested to see if cats really do land on
their feet.

The other half muttered something about an
urgent appointment and began to sidle off to the
bar, but our man with the tractor had other ideas.
"You must get a ladder," he said, "and recuperate
the cat while I go to fetch Madame Noiret. *Allez!*
We shall return with all speed." And away he trotted
on his errand of mercy.

With much dragging of the feet, the other half
went to the garage and came back with an extension
ladder, which for once he managed to erect without
mutilating his fingers. He wedged it up into the tree,
cursing the while, with madame telling him to be
careful and moderate his language with the cat. As
he climbed the ladder, the top of the tree began to
bend in a most promising manner, with ginger Tom
clinging on like grim death and hissing furiously.

I was well placed to see what happened next. The
other half made reassuring noises and stretched out
a rescuing hand, which was promptly attacked by

tooth and claw. Ungrateful beasts, cats, as I've always
maintained, and the other half had one or two choice
phrases to describe them as he returned to earth with
scratches up to his elbow, just in time to welcome
Madame Noiret and her henchman.

She, of course, was in a fine old state about it all,
wringing her hands and wailing and calling out to
her little ray of sunshine in the branches to calm himself, *Maman* was here, double rations of calves' liver
for dinner if he came down, and so forth. But he
wasn't having any of it, and after seeing the damage
to the other half's arm, there was a distinct shortage
of volunteers to climb up and get him.

If I'd been in charge, I'd have left him there until
autumn, when he would have dropped off with the
leaves, but Madame Noiret was working herself into
a lather of distress. "It's all your fault," said she to
the other half. "It's your dog who has terrorized my
poor Zouzou. What are you going to do?"

To which he replied—reasonably enough, I
thought, after being wounded in action—"Madame,
your cat was in my garage. My ladder is at your dis-
posal. I'm going to bandage my arm, and then I shall
very probably have a drink to restore myself. Good
day to you."

This wouldn't do at all. Madame Noiret puffed
herself up like an irate balloon and then demanded to
use the telephone. In the face of such inhuman behavior, she said, she was forced to invoke the highest
authorities. The English may have no regard for

helpless animals, or so she claimed, but the French, being civilized, certainly do. We shall summon the *pompiers* and let the brave lads of the fire department save Zouzou.

Anything for a quiet life is the management's motto, and so into the house they all went to make the call and glare at one another. I had become rather bored by now, and I went off digging with the Labrador to pass the time until the arrival of the boys in blue, with their cranes and, I hoped, hydraulically operated cat extractors. It's very modern, the French fire department, and I had a mental picture of Zouzou being plucked off his branch by giant forceps.

But as things turned out, it wasn't exactly the joyful climax you might have expected. The *pompiers* duly turned up, and we all went down to the drive to welcome them, Madame Noiret leading the way with cries of relief, showering blessings on anyone wearing a uniform, and pointing the finger of scorn at the other half. A bossy, disagreeable old boot, she was, and thoroughly deserving of what came next.

The captain cut her off in midbabble and asked her where the endangered cat was. "Follow me," said Madame Noiret. "Bring your men and suitable equipment. And *vite!* There is not a moment to be lost."

The procession made its way up to the almond tree, with Madame Noiret calling out in that nauseating way people address their cats, and then there was

The tree was uninhabited.

what you could only describe as a pregnant and embarrassed silence. The tree was uninhabited. Zouzou, finally showing a vestige of common sense, had gone while the going was good and we were all otherwise engaged.

The best was yet to come. Madame Noiret, having made the call, was obliged to pay for bringing out the assembled forces of the fire department without due cause. She protested and carried on, as I've noticed people do when their wallets are under threat, but it was to no avail. The captain made the bill out on the spot.

The other half was smiling for the rest of the day, despite his wounds.

The Tasting

*I*f, like me, you have a logical turn of mind, a self-indulgent nature, and a frequently dormant conscience, there is a certain aspect of human behavior that can put an immense strain on the patience. It's spoken of, always in sanctimonious tones, as moderation—not too much of this, not too much of that, diet and abstinence and restraint, colonic irrigation, cold baths before breakfast, and regular readings of morally uplifting tracts. You must have come across all this and worse if you have any friends from California. Personally, I'm a great believer in the philosophy of live and let live, as long as you keep your proclivities to yourself. Follow the road of denial if that's what you want, and all I'll say is more fool you and spare me the details.

Unfortunately, you can't avoid self-righteousness altogether, and this curious distrust of pleasure is

nowhere more apparent than in the matter of drink.
People like to drink. This became obvious to me very
shortly after I arrived at the house of a thousand
bottles (most of them empty). But it is rarely the simple, spontaneous process it should be, because there
is always the question of the clock. I can't tell you
how often I've noticed it: When offered a drink, what
is the first thing most people do? Look at their
watches, as if the hour had anything to do with thirst.
They invariably accept, but never before a token
display of reluctance, usually dispelled by invoking
the support of international time zones. Someone,
somewhere in the world, is nursing a stiff one on the
rocks. This apparently provides the necessary seal of
approval.

Then there are the excuses, although I don't know
why they bother; I never need an excuse to jump in
and make a beast of myself. But they do, and they'll
clutch at any straw. Birthdays, weddings and wakes,
the arrival of a new year, the departure of the mother-
in-law, the anniversary of the death of Napoleon's
favorite horse—the list is long and ingenious, and
I've seen the bottles tumble for no other reason than
the sighting of the first cuckoo. In my experience,
however, there is no excuse quite as transparent as
the wine tasting, a clear case of wretched excess
thinly disguised as education, if you ask me. But
you'd better read on and judge for yourself.

The hero of the occasion was a little fellow with
bandy legs and a pocketful of corkscrews, who was

I never need an excuse to plunge in.

known to his admirers as Gaston the Nose. He
supplies many of the local residents with wine that
he claims is grown on his family estate and available
only to the privileged few. This always goes down
well with the landed gentry, who tend to believe anything that flatters them, and they also like his accom-
modating habit of bringing supplies to the house,
thus avoiding the unsteady drive back after a few
liquid hours at the vineyard.

I'm not sure how Gaston did it—bribery, I
wouldn't wonder—but one fine day he had somehow
persuaded the management to throw open the doors
of the stately home and provide a convenient venue

for a *dégustation extraordinaire*. Friends were invited, with the kickoff at twelve noon, and don't forget your checkbook. The whole idea, you see, being to render the clientele softheaded and in a mood to place extravagant orders.

Gaston arrived early to prepare for the event. As I've said, he's a small man—apart from his nose, which is impressive—and it was like watching an agitated jockey looking for his horse as he scampered in and out fetching his treasures. He set them out on the table: rows of bottles, oversized glasses, small spitting buckets, and napkins for those inclined to dribble. And then out came the ceremonial corkscrew, and he started crooning to himself as he opened the bottles. Every one was a little marvel, according to him, and he kept on dashing into the kitchen to wave corks under madame's nose while she was doing her best to get the rations organized. The other half even took a break from his pencil sharpening to lend a hand, and in no time the dining room took on the appearance of a refreshment stand at the village fete.

Thirst must encourage punctuality, I suppose, because by noon the students of the grape were present and assembled. Familiar faces, most of them—Eloise, the artist with watercolorist's block; the woman who breeds snails farther up the valley and her husband, the drinker with the writing problem; Angus, the Scottish refugee; Jules and Jim from the village; and the visiting expert, Charles, an English gentleman from the wine trade, complete with grog-blossom complexion—in other words, a representative selection of the dregs of local society, champing at the bit for the first glass of the day.

It was hot outside, and so I decided to stay in the shade under the table and hope for the odd contribution from above. Madame had been giving her all in the kitchen, and among other delights on offer were pâtés, salami, ham, tarts of various persuasions, and cheeses. From past experience, I know that wine makes for careless hands. Fingers lose their grasp, and there is usually a choice of low-flying delicacies for those who lie in wait. Alas, nothing in life is without its price, and in this case I was obliged to listen to some of the most arrant twaddle I'd heard since I gave up the struggle with television.

It began quietly enough, with Gaston twittering on about the rules of *dégustation,* the importance of following procedure so that the palate is primed to appreciate the developing subtleties of taste, the crucial role of the nostrils, and a few other gems of mumbo jumbo. This was followed by a brief period of silence, presumably while the assembled tasters were performing their devotions over their glasses, and then—this actually made me sit up, because I thought the plumbing had taken a turn for the worse—the sound effects took over.

Swilling, that's the word. They swilled in unison; they gurgled; they made prolonged sucking noises. And they spat. I've known children sent to bed in disgrace for far less offensive behavior at the table, but they seemed to be highly delighted with themselves, little Gaston congratulating them on what he called their "professional technique." Mind you, he'd probably have said the same if they'd chosen to drink stark naked through a straw as long as they came through with an order at the end of the day. Praise from a salesman, in my humble opinion, is one of life's less convincing compliments.

The sounds of suction continued apace, although I noticed that as time passed the level of spitting dropped off sharply. And then, after a particularly prolonged and noisy session of squelches and gargles, we were given the benefit of some learned comments from Charles, the gentleman in the wine trade. "Brambles," he said, "truffles, spices, a hint of weasel, bewildering complexity, but"—and this brought the house down, so you can tell that they were quite well on by now—"isn't it a little young to be up so late?"

"*Mais non,*" piped Gaston, drawing himself up to his full height, such as it was. "This wine is delightfully precocious. He has body, legs, shoulders, stamina, a pedigree, a formidable personality. Also, he has ambition." And with that, glasses were refilled while the other connoisseurs joined in the debate.

It had the makings of rather an interesting squabble, with the French contingent closing ranks against the English "milord." He started looking down his

The informed nose

nose, and made the mistake of talking about the glories of Bordeaux, which was a gift to our side, of course. Jules and Jim asked him, with a great deal of sniggering, how this year's vintage was in Wimbledon, and the discussion was degenerating quite promisingly when Eloise came out of her trance. "The spirit of the wine," said she, "is definitely burnt umber. I can see it. There's an aura. Artists can sense these things." This, mark you, coming from someone who hadn't laid hand on brush in living memory.

In less exalted company, of course, a remark like that would have been treated as a sure sign of the third level of intoxication, and Eloise would have been sent off to a dark room with smelling salts and a glass of water. But amazingly enough, the assembled sages took it seriously, and my hopes of a noisy rift in international relations vanished as they settled down to discuss the aura of wines. I ask you.

Student of the human condition though I may be, there's a limit to the amount of pretentious nonsense I can listen to, and it was by now time for my afternoon stroll. This is usually taken in the company of the management, but they were rooted to their seats with fixed and glassy grins as the conversation became ever more fatuous, and so I decided to leave them to fend for themselves.

A solitary expedition quite suited me, in fact, because I had for some time been planning to visit a neighboring farmhouse where a new dog had taken up residence. I'd seen her from the forest path. A fetching little thing, she was, too, small but perfectly formed, and I would have dropped in to pay my respects earlier if the management hadn't dragged me away. And so I left the brain trust to their deliberations and slipped out of the house. An assignation in the vines, I thought, would be just the thing to clear the head after the intellectual rigors of a wine tasting.

One doesn't rush on these occasions. Call me old-fashioned if you like, but I don't believe in arriving for a tryst panting for breath and with the tongue hanging out. It doesn't do to appear too eager. Besides, I never hurry through the forest, for fear of missing something. I prefer to prowl, all senses alert, the master of the wilderness and scourge of small things that squeak.

It changes every day, you know, the forest, perhaps not to the eye of man, but certainly to the informed nose. You can smell where hunting dogs have been, if a wild boar has crossed the path, whether or not the rabbits have been out and about, as well as the traces of human passage. And, below it all, the dry, sharp smell of pine needles and wild herbs mingling, on a good day, with the bouquet of a stale ham sandwich left behind by a passing hiker. Full of surprises, nature.

I made my way in a long loop through the trees, darting hither and yon as sounds and scents demanded my attention, until I came to a vantage point on a slope above the farmhouse. I looked down, and there was my sleeping beauty, tethered in the shade and snoring gently, the picture of innocence. Well, I thought, we'll soon put an end to that, but I held back for a moment—not out of any gallant or romantic feelings, to be honest, but so that I could make sure there wasn't some dangerous clod with a gun lurking in the wings.

The coast was clear, and I approached on noiseless paw. On close inspection, she was smaller than I had thought, but nicely rounded, with a fresh young smell to her and a charming little beard. I woke her up with a searching nudge to the rump. She jumped to her feet, yelped, bit me, and wedged herself behind a large flowerpot—all the signs, in case you're not familiar with them, of instant attraction. Strange indeed are the ways of love.

We dallied. Or rather, I did my best to dally, and she eventually began to enter into the spirit of things, but there was a serious obstacle. I was twice her height, and without artificial assistance, there was no way in which we could relate, if you follow me. It's vital to remember this, in light of subsequent events, but you can take my word for it: The inclination was there, but practical considerations intervened.

I don't give up without a struggle, and as dusk fell I was still trying to apply logic to the problem when the interlude ended on a dramatic note. Ah, you'll be thinking, the earth finally moved. Not a bit of it. I was

so preoccupied that I had no idea we were being
observed until I felt a thunderous kick in the ribs and
heard the furious cries of the proprietor, who had
staggered home from his needlework class to find
us in what he assumed, with his dirty mind, was
flagrante delicto.

It was not a moment for loitering. I retreated to my
vantage point on the slope behind the house, con-
cealed myself behind a bush, and pondered. So near
and yet so far, I thought. Star-crossed lovers sepa-
rated by a cruel twist of fate, unfulfilled yearning,
and, as though that weren't enough for one day, I was
beginning to feel an overpowering hollowness, which
reminded me that I'd missed lunch. As dusk turned
into night, I started back home, bittersweet memories giving way to anticipation of what might be waiting for me in the kitchen. I'm not one for pining—at
least, not on an empty stomach.

The forest is not normally a busy place after dark,
and so I was surprised to see gleams of flashlights
ahead of me, on the path and in the trees. I paused.
Caution is the thing when you come across strangers
in the night. They might be hunters, and I had no
desire to be mistaken for something edible. Accidents happen from time to time, and it has been
known for hunters to shoot first and apologize later,
as they did with Madame Noiret's cat only the other
day. She took it rather badly, but for once nobody
could blame me.

I made a detour off the path until I was safely above

the flashlights, and in the flickers of light I made out a group of figures. They were blundering through the undergrowth, bumping into trees and tripping gracefully over rocks, or sitting down with that peculiar, sudden jerk caused by the legs giving way with no prior warning. It was when one of them cried out in pain after choosing a sharp place to sit that I recognized the voice, and as I came closer, I saw that it was indeed Gaston the Nose, with his merry band of connoisseurs around him. The program for the day obviously included a nature ramble after the wine tasting.

I thought I'd join in for a few minutes before going home, and I went up behind Gaston as he was massaging his injury, barking politely to make myself known.

What a welcome. All thoughts of his wound behind him, Gaston called out to the others—Name of a pipe, it is Boy; I have found him. Madame will be ravished, heaven be praised, and a lot more besides—and amid the patting and chirruping and general excitement, I realized that this was in fact a search party sent out to look for yours truly. They'd probably still be there now if I hadn't found them, but that's beside the point. I was rather touched by their concern, actually, and made sure they were all present and correct before I guided them home.

Madame was duly ravished to see me again, and, after a few moments of halfhearted scolding, dinner was served. Very good, it was, too, with the bonus of some chicken sautéed in Marsala (which I'm very partial to) as an aid to recovery at the end of a trying day. And that, you might think, should have been followed by a dive into the basket and lights out.

But it wasn't, and here I return to earlier remarks about drink needing an excuse, however flimsy. My safe return from nameless horrors was treated as cause for celebration, and damned if the valiant wine tasters didn't make for the bottles again, little Gaston leading the way with rampant corkscrew, and the rest of them crowding around like camels after a month in the Sahara. The last thing I remember hearing before nodding off under the table was that rosé doesn't travel, but I wouldn't take that too much to heart. The good ones do.

Ordeal by Chicken

*T*here are magical mornings in life when the sun catches the treetops, there's a nip in the air and dew underfoot, every prospect pleases, and one enjoys a special sense of well-being. Frisky, if you know what I mean, and ready to pounce. On mornings such as these, with the blood coursing through the veins, I like to take a turn through the vineyard in the hope of finding something small and unimportant to terrify. I'm told that this takes place frequently in the corridors of large business corporations when the chairman of the board makes his rounds, beating the bushes for vice presidents and junior executives and generally making himself giddy with power. It's the same principle, you see, except that in my case, I'm on the lookout for fur and feather instead of dark suits.

The vineyard was cool and damp, the head-high

green tunnels stretching away over the hill, and, for once, not a hunter in sight. I've never had much time for hunters, as you know, mainly because their lack of stealth spoils everything for the rest of us. A single prowling hunter makes enough noise as he tiptoes through the fields to scare off every living thing between here and the other side of the mountain. Heaven knows how those who spend the winter asleep get a moment's peace with all the stamping and cursing that goes on. Perhaps our hibernating friends are becoming progressively deaf. It's wonderful how nature adapts to changed circumstances.

As this profound thought came to me, I saw a clutch of chickens at the end of the vines and paused for a moment to muse further on the evolutionary process. Here we have a bird with wings who is incapable of sustained flight and whose sole accomplishments are the cackle and the indiscriminate laying of eggs. Odd, when you think about it. And on that puzzling note, I put reflection aside and became the beast of prey, moving like a ghost toward my intended victims.

There must have been four or five of them, and they were scratching at the earth and jerking their heads up and down—not unlike humans overtaken by the urge to dance, in fact—when I sprang from cover and made for what looked like the slowest old boiler of the group.

Away she went with the others, showing a surpris-

ing swiftness out of the starting gate, screeching
and carrying on as if I already had my teeth clamped
around her vitals, and we cleared the vines in racing
style. I suppose if the question before you is to run
faster or have your head bitten off, it tends to give
you that added impetus. All I can say is that those
chickens were covering the ground like thorough-
breds, and I was still a few yards behind them when
they shot under a stone arch and into the courtyard
of a ramshackle farm. Now I had them, I thought to
myself. A chicken in a confined space is a chicken in
trouble. And so, speed no longer being of the
essence, I sauntered in after them to make my selection for the day.

Never count your chickens, as I believe Voltaire
used to say, and how right he was. They were there,
sure enough, but so was an unpleasant-looking old
fellow standing next to a pile of logs, chain saw in his
hand, mad glint in his eye, complexion like a beet-
root, cloth cap and boots. I recognized the type from
my youth, a living warning of the dangers of inter-
breeding and too much cheap red wine for breakfast.
How the authorities can allow them to wander at
liberty amazes me, but there we are.

I assumed a nonchalant air, as though I'd been
taking a harmless stroll with no thought in my head
of molesting his precious brood, and nodded at him.
He glared back and then looked at the old boiler.
She had collapsed in a corner of the courtyard and
seemed to be having some difficulty breathing.

I assumed a nonchalant air.

Chickens aren't designed for the extended sprint, you see, and the effort and excitement had clearly taken its toll.

Well, you could almost hear the machinery whirring in his head as he strained to analyze the situation. He finally made the mental leap that there might be a causal relationship between my presence and the chicken in distress, put down his chain saw, and reached for the nearest log. I'm never slow to take a hint, and so I did a brisk about-face and headed for the vines. When I stopped to look back, he was standing in the entrance to the courtyard, watching me, log in hand and, I suspected, unkind thoughts in his head. I made a mental note to keep a safe distance between us in the future.

You can imagine my alarm that evening when there was a hammering on the door, and who should be standing on the threshold with thunderous brow but the proud guardian of the chickens. He had come to see the management, and from the initial exchanges, it didn't appear to be a social visit.

But, to give credit where it's due, the management did their best to be gracious, asking him to come in, offering him a drink, and pretending to ignore the trail of mud, straw, and droppings that he left on the floor. I stayed tactfully out of sight in the kitchen, ears flapping, and listened.

Introductions were made, and Roussel, as he called himself, launched into his tale of woe. That morning, he said, he had suffered the grievous loss of his most productive chicken—a chicken, furthermore, that he had nurtured from egg to magnificent maturity and had become very attached to, a chicken of rare character and affectionate disposition, a veritable queen among chickens. This priceless specimen had turned up her toes as the result of a heart attack. Roussel snuffled into his drink for a moment or two to let us appreciate the full tragedy of his bereavement.

The management made polite sounds of shock and horror, but I could tell they had no idea why they were being included in the mourning party. I knew what was coming, of course, and it didn't take long.

Roussel allowed himself to be pressed into another drink, held back the tears manfully, and got down to

The full tragedy of his bereavement

business. The heart attack that had cut short the life of one of nature's most noble achievements had been caused by overexertion, he said, while trying to escape the merciless jaws of a savage and untrained dog. A dog, alas, that lived in this very house. *Beh oui.* In this very house.

I retreated farther into the kitchen while the penny dropped. The management, quite rightly in my view, asked Roussel for some evidence. After all, they said, there were dozens of dogs in the valley, most of them with criminal records of one kind or another. What made him so sure that the finger of suspicion was pointing in the right direction?

"Ah," said Roussel, leaning forward and exercising his eyebrows furiously, "but I have seen this dog in my own courtyard. I can describe him to you." Which he proceeded to do, and I have to say that the experience of listening to a biased, vindictive old liar blackening my character and making unflattering remarks about my physical appearance was not something I'd care to go through again. He was a shameless embroiderer, apart from anything else, claiming that he had seen me with a mouthful of feathers on the morning in question. Why not throw in a napkin and a knife and fork while you're at it, I thought, and I'm sure he would have mentioned them had the thought occurred to him. It was barefaced perjury, nothing less, and I couldn't believe that he'd get away with it.

But, what do you know, he did. The management took it all in, with occasional gasps of horror from madame, and the other half up and down every five minutes with the conciliatory bottle. A sickening display, in my opinion. They should have thrown him out.

Instead—you'll hardly believe this, but it's true— they finished up by paying him for the loss of his old boiler, which was what he'd wanted from the start, I'm sure, and when he finally put on his cap to go home, they were chatting away like bosom friends. And there it should have ended, with a minor rebuke for yours truly and no hard feelings. But no.

Fortified by drink and made expansive, no doubt, by a sudden rush of money to the pocket, Roussel stopped at the door and offered a suggestion that made the blood run cold. "Your dog," he said, "could be trained for chickens. There is a way that never fails, and since you have been so understanding in my hour of grief, it will be my pleasure to teach him."

There are moments in life when you can see retribution and disaster coming from afar and be powerless to avoid them. I tried everything—the full range of blandishments, limping awkwardly, a coughing fit, trembling under the bed—but to no avail. The management had been bamboozled by the old sadist into believing that he was interested in contributing to my further education. But it was quite plain to me: A generous financial settlement wasn't enough for him; he wanted revenge. I've heard the same said about divorce.

The following morning, appropriately, was overcast and gray as I was dragged across the fields to Roussel's training academy and delivered into the hands of my professor. He told the management to come back in an hour, when, so he said, they would find a changed dog, free of all vicious habits and cured forever of chicken addiction. And do you know what? They actually thanked him. Defies belief, doesn't it? Rare jewels, the management, but I sometimes wonder about their competence in the matter of character assessment.

Roussel took me into a shed and closed the door. I was immediately reminded of my first home, even down to the mud floor and the decorative accessories. It was a cramped, grimy place, littered with family heirlooms—rusty buckets, an ancient bicycle, rotting sacks, split barrels, and a variety of prehistoric implements that Roussel was obviously saving to pass on to his grateful grandchildren. I looked around for possible avenues of escape, and found myself hypnotized by the sight of the old boiler of yesterday, now very much the worse for wear, flat out on a tin table. Her head, with its wilted wattles, was hanging over the edge, and one lifeless eye fixed me with a mournful stare. A grim tableau, you might say, and so it was, but I couldn't understand why she was there and not simmering peacefully on the stove. Even the old ones are quite tasty, you know, if you cook them long enough.

Roussel picked her up by the legs and swung her to and fro—showing no respect for the dear departed, I remember thinking—and then came over and held the body toward me for inspection. Out of courtesy more than genuine interest, I leaned forward for a closer look, whereupon he whirled it up and very nearly succeeded in scoring a direct hit on my head. In fact, the beak just nicked me on the snout as I pulled away, and very painful it was, too.

It was then that I understood the nature of the lesson. In his simpleminded fashion, Roussel was hoping that a few blows from a blunt feathered instrument would overcome instincts that had been developed over generations. Futile, of course, but he wasn't to know that, and he came after me again, chicken flailing away, while I ducked and dodged as best I could. It's a measure of the man's stupidity that it took him some considerable time to realize I would be an easier target if I was tethered.

There was an extended break in hostilities while he searched the shed for a chain or a rope, becoming more and more ill-tempered as he delved among the relics while I kept as far from him as space allowed. Eventually, he must have remembered where he kept his supply of string—probably in a safe under his bed—and he left the shed, grunting horribly, shutting the door and leaving me alone with the dead chicken.

Desperate situations require desperate remedies. You may remember that I told you the shed had a mud floor, and I took advantage of Roussel's absence to dig away in the corner until I'd made a grave of sufficient size to conceal all of the chicken except one obstinate leg, which wouldn't stay down. Rigor mortis had set in, I think, or perhaps pressure of time prevented me from digging deep enough. In any case, it wasn't a problem, because I sat on the burial mound to conceal the protruding limb, and that is how Roussel found me when he returned with a length of rope.

There was a flaw in my scheme, which the more attentive among you have probably noticed, and it was revealed when Roussel approached to tie me up. I moved out of the corner to keep away from him, and the chicken's upright leg was left in full view.

I wish you'd seen the expression on his face, but I'll spare you the language. Suffice it to say that he was taken aback. Throwing down the rope, he knelt down to unearth the body so that lessons could continue. This was the picture—Roussel scrabbling in the dirt, backside presented to the door—that greeted the management as they arrived to collect me.

I didn't stay to witness the rest of it. As soon as the door opened, I was out, back across the fields and home, with nothing more to show for the experience than a superficial beak wound. When the management returned, all was forgiven, as it usually is, and I'm delighted to say that the budding social life with Roussel seems to have come to an abrupt end. I see him on the horizon occasionally, and he hurls a stone in my direction for old time's sake, but accuracy isn't his strong point.

Did I learn anything from it all? Certainly: Never approach a man armed with a dead chicken. There's something similar in a slim volume called *The Art of War* about avoiding conflict with superior forces. Sun Tzu is the author, in case you're interested.

The Joy of Balls

A friend of the family who descends on us from ·
time to time is one of the few people I know
who shares my habit of relaxing under the
dining table. Not for him the stiff formality of the
chair and polite social intercourse. On occasion,
once he has eaten, he has been known to slide gently
down to join me, and we bond. You may find this
hard to believe, but there are photographs in existence to prove it. He maintains that it helps his
digestion, although I feel it has more to do with a
longing for quiet and serene company after all the
conversational cut-and-thrust that takes place on the
top deck. In any event, he is a kindred spirit.

It happens that he is also some kind of eminence in
the world of British tennis—head ball boy at the
Queen's Club, it may be, or possibly a senior catering
executive, I'm not sure. Whatever it is, his position

gives him access to the highest levels of the annual Queen's Tournament. He rubs shoulders with players and royalty and is permitted to use the VIP toilet facilities, which apparently is an honor reserved for the fortunate few. All this, I learned in the course of a long session under the table after lunch one day.

As I may have mentioned, I do like to have something to chew when the mood takes me, live preferably, but that involves catching it first, and for some reason it's not too popular with the management. And so, faute de mieux, I usually have to make do with an inanimate object such as a stick, the Labrador's blanket, or a guest's shoe. Dull pickings, for the most part, although I did manage to get hold of a child's teddy bear once. It didn't put up much of a fight, I have to say, and there were tearful recrimi-

*I like to have something to chew when
the mood takes me.*

Not up to championship standards

nations over the remains, much wailing and gnashing of teeth, followed by solitary confinement for the winner. The stuffing gave me a bilious attack, too. Everything these days are man-made fibers, which I can tell you are highly indigestible. If you've ever eaten squid in a cheap Italian restaurant, you'll know what I mean.

It was shortly after the teddy bear incident that I was given my first tennis ball, and I took to it immediately. Round, springy, and small enough to carry in one side of the mouth while barking from the other, it was my constant companion for weeks. You can imagine my hurt feelings, therefore, when the refugee from Queen's arrived one day, took a look at my ball, and sneered. "Not up to championship standards," he said. "Furthermore, it's bald, soiled, and out of shape." Well, you could say the same about quite a few of the guests whom I've seen come and go, but I'm not one for the gratuitous insult. Goodwill to all men is my rule in life, as long as they make themselves useful with the biscuits.

I had more or less recovered from the disparaging remarks about my recreational equipment when what should arrive at the house but a large box, addressed to me. This was unusual enough for the postman to come in and deliver it by hand, together with some facetious and quite unnecessary comments about my inability to sign for it. While he was congratulating himself on his feeble witticism, I took the opportunity to go and lift my leg on a sackful of undelivered mail that he'd left outside the door. Revenge is damp.

I came back to find the box open and the management studying a letter that described the pedigree of the contents. These were tennis balls, dozens of them, barely marked and with full heads of bright yellow fur. But they were not just everyday balls. According to the letter, they were balls of tremendous importance and fame, having appeared on television. They had been used in the men's finals of the Queen's Tournament and collected, still warm from their exertions, by our man on the spot and sent over for my personal use.

To begin with, I just sat and looked at them, and gloated. After being rationed to a single ball, a whole box of them gave me a delightful feeling of sudden wealth. French politicians must have a similar sensation when elected to high office and permitted to dip into the châteaux and limousines and government-issue caviar. No wonder they cling to power long after they should be tucked away in an old folks' home. I'd do the same.

I was sorting through the balls before selecting my playmate for the day when I was struck by an interesting difference in the messages they were sending to the nose. If you've ever watched tennis—I'm sure some people do when they have nothing better to amuse themselves—you will have noticed that the contestants always keep a couple of spare balls in the pocket of their shorts. In this dark, overheated space, some kind of osmosis occurs, and the balls take on the character of the athletic and perspiring thigh. And if you happen to possess, as I do, a sensitive and highly tuned sense of smell, it's possible to identify the thigh's owner—not by name, of course, but by place of origin.

I applied the deductive faculties and was able to divide the balls into two groups. On the left was the Old World—complex, mature, with a long Teutonic finish and a hint of alcohol-free beer. On the right,

I applied deductive faculties.

a clear signal from the Dark Continent, hot and dusty, with a refreshing tang of the high veldt. Now, as I said, I can't give you names, but if you go back over the records, I think you'll find the finalists for that year were German and South African. Advantage, *moi*. Fascinating, isn't it?

And that, in my considered opinion, is one of the few interesting aspects of tennis. As in much of what passes for sport, a basic principle has been misunderstood. The essence of any game, it seems to me, is to gain possession of the ball and find a quiet corner where one can destroy it in peace. But what do we see these highly paid and luridly dressed people doing with the ball? They hit it, kick it, throw it, bounce it, put it in a net, put it in a hole, and generally play the fool with it. Then they either kiss each other and slap hands or have a tantrum and go and mope in the corner. Adult men and women they are, too, although you'd never guess it. I've known five-year-olds with a better grip on themselves.

But I wouldn't want you to think that I'm completely devoid of sporting instincts. My own version of fetch the ball, for example, provides me with hours of harmless enjoyment and keeps participating adults away from the bar and out of mischief. I always win, too, which is as it should be.

First, I choose an elevated spot. It could be the top of a flight of stairs, a wall, the raised edge of the swimming pool—anywhere that gives me a height advantage. Stairs are best, because of the added cardiovascular benefits, but I shall come to that in a minute.

I take up my position, ball in mouth, and lurk with lowered head, in the manner of the vulture contemplating the imminent death of his breakfast. Sooner or later, this motionless and rather extraordinary pose attracts attention. "What is Boy doing?" they say. Or, "Is he going to be sick?" With the eyes of the assembled spectators upon me, I slowly open my mouth and let the ball bounce free. Down the steps, off the wall, or into the deep end it goes. I remain completely still, the unblinking eye fixed on the ball below me. It is a tense and focused moment.

The tension lasts until someone has the common sense to grasp the purpose of the game, which is to

A tense and focused moment

retrieve the ball and return it to me. If the spectators are particularly dense—and I've known a few, believe me, who didn't seem to know whether it was lunchtime or Tuesday—I might have to give a short bark to indicate start of play. The ball is fetched, brought back, and presented to me. I give the players a minute or two to settle down and get over the excitement, and then I repeat the process.

I mentioned stairs earlier. These have the double attraction of noise and healthy physical exertion, in contrast to the visitors' usual program of elbow bending and free-weight training with knife and fork. The falling ball provides multiple bouncing sounds, and the retriever has to climb up the stairs to give it back to me. As any doctor will tell you, this is very beneficial for the legs and lungs.

The Joy of Balls

I'll admit, though, that there have been days when I've been off form with the long game. Balls take unlucky bounces, as we all know, and sometimes get lost in the rough. Or, more often, the spectators have been too preoccupied with refreshments to pay attention. And here, I think, is an inspirational example of dedication and the will to win coming through against all odds.

It was one of those evenings when nothing I could do impinged on the happy hour. I lurked, I dropped, I barked, and still the merriment continued. I even suffered the ignominy of having to fetch the ball myself—which, as any of those tennis people will tell you, is a fate worse than having to pay for your own rackets. But instead of bursting into tears and calling for the manager, as most of *them* do, I brought out my short game.

The assembled guests—there must have been eight or ten of them in varying stages of incoherence—were all seated around a low table, bleating away about the hardships of life as they punished the hors d'oeuvres and held out their empty glasses for more of the same. None of them noticed me as I slipped, wraith-like, through the forest of legs and arms to the table.

Then—overhead smash!—I dropped the ball into a bowl of tapenade, which, as you may know, is a dark, oily dip made from olives. It splatters in a most satisfying way, and those in the immediate vicinity came out in a black rash.

You could have heard a jaw drop. It was well worth

the retribution that followed, and to this day, whenever I pick up my ball of choice, I am regarded with the wary respect befitting a champion. Incidentally, if you've never tried tapenade-flavored tennis ball, I can recommend it. Recipe on request.

The Girl Next Door

I am not easily embarrassed. I am at ease in crowded rooms, comfortable with strangers, and, I like to think, modest and gracious in the face of compliments—with one exception.

"Look at Boy. He's just like one of the family." If I've heard that idiotic phrase once, I've heard it a hundred times, and it never fails to make me cringe. The question I ask myself is, Which one? It can't be madame, because of the difference in gender, so I presume I am being compared with the other half, and if anyone thinks that's a compliment, they've picked the wrong dog. The other half is an admirable fellow in many ways, a prince among walkers and a generous hand at feeding times. But he'd be the first to admit that he's shortsighted, devoid of facial hair, poorly coordinated, useless with rabbits, and given to prolonged bouts of idleness. You know me well

enough by now, I'm sure, to understand my lack of
enthusiasm for the comparison.

Mind you, there is something to be said for the
theory that certain people and certain dogs share
personality defects, and even the odd physical quirk,
and this was brought home to me not long ago when
we entertained Sven, the diminutive Swede, and his
repellent corgi, Ingmar. I should say here, before
anyone from the Swedish Anti-Defamation League
takes umbrage, that when it comes to Swedes in general, I am not averse—pleasant people on the whole,
and they make a good topless sandwich.

Sven, however, is a monster in everything but
size—aggressive, dictatorial, self-important, noisy,
and smug. He also has extremely short legs and a
strut. Now, the more perceptive among you will have
realized that this description, from the aggression to
the strut, could easily be applied to the corgi, which
we all know is one of nature's wasted efforts. And to
see the similarity between the two of them, Sven and
Ingmar, yapping in unison and mincing up and
down together, was truly uncanny. The other half
must have noticed it, too, because when he appeared
with a hospitable vodka in one hand and a dog biscuit
in the other, there was a moment's confusion before
he could decide who got what.

But I digress. What I was going to tell you may
come as a surprise, since you may have guessed that
I dislike most dogs who operate very close to the
ground. I won't deny it—they get under your feet,

and they have a tendency to nip—but there are always exceptions, and I found my thoughts returning more and more often to the shy little jewel I had recently met, the girl next door with the beard. Over the weeks that followed, I slipped away whenever the chance presented itself in the hope that we could find a solution to our earlier problem. The course of true love is often strewn with obstacles, as the Pekinese discovered when he formed a romantic attachment to a cushion, but I was convinced that ingenuity would win through in the end.

Experienced generals and burglars will always tell you that reconnaissance is the key to success, and I spent many hours behind my bush above the farmhouse, observing the comings and goings and waiting for the *moment juste*. The same routine was followed each morning, with the lady of the house taking my intended—Fifine, she was called, if I overheard correctly—for a decorous stroll in the field before tethering her by the back door. I decided to test the defenses one day, and I issued a haunting love call from behind the bush. Fifine pricked up her ears and it seemed that she blew a kiss in my general direction, but I was barely halfway down the slope before the door opened and a vision of nastiness appeared, waving a carving knife and snarling.

And so it went on, with my sorties toward Fifine consistently foiled by the old bat in the kitchen, and then something happened that dampened the ardor and made me think I might have better luck elsewhere. It was the hour of the aperitif, when the proprietor was in the habit of resting from his labors with a glass under the shade of a tree. Occasionally, he would let Fifine off her rope, and the two of them would contemplate the sunset together, although why she chose to stay at his feet when I was available, I'll never understand. There's no accounting for female behavior. All over you one minute and keep your distance the next, in my experience. I'm told it has something to do with the moon.

Anyway, there they were under the tree when who should emerge from the back door but Professor Roussel of the chicken academy, accompanied by a dog that looked as though he'd come from a long line of rodents—portly, short of leg, narrow of snout, and thoroughly unattractive. You've seen the type on rabies posters. It was obvious that they all knew one another, because the two men settled down with a bottle while Fifine and fatty gamboled in the grass. That was a blow in itself, but far worse was to come.

The two men were sucking down the cough mixture and deep in conversation, so they failed to notice what I could see clearly. Fifine, who was showing all the signs of being a forward little hussy, was luring her companion away from the tree and around to the side of the house—darting toward him, leaping over him (not difficult), rolling on her back, and then scuttling away. Crude provocation of a sexual nature, there's no other way to describe it. She might just as well have taken him by the scruff of his neck and dragged him off. I found the spectacle deeply offensive, but you know how it is when something horrible but fascinating is taking place; you can't stop watching.

Delicacy compels me to draw a veil over what I saw next, except to say that Fifine had her way with him behind a rosebush before returning to her master's feet, looking like Miss Prim after a strenuous game of croquet. Dreams shattered, heart broken, anguished and distraught, I returned home. Luckily, I found where the old Labrador had buried a marrowbone, so the day wasn't entirely wasted. Even so, it had been an emotional setback, and it confirmed all my feelings about dogs with short legs. Slaves of instant gratification, if you ask me, and very lacking in discrimination. I crossed Fifine off my list of future attractions, and resolved to find a more suitable com-

Dreams shattered

panion, perhaps one of the Doberman sisters I see on Sunday mornings in the forest, or perhaps both of them. I'm not selfish.

It was well into autumn before I was reminded of Fifine, and a most unpleasant reminder it was, too. For once, the evening was free of social engagements, and we were *en famille*—fire blazing, dinner coming along nicely in the kitchen, the two old bitches whiffling away in their baskets—when there was a knock on the door. The management doesn't take kindly to unexpected interruptions like this at feeding time, and there is always considerable reluctance to welcome the unknown visitor. Madame raises her eyes to heaven, the other half mutters curses, and I've known them both to go and hide in the bedroom, pretending to be out. But the knocking continued, and the other half was dispatched to send the intruder packing.

He failed miserably, as he often does—I'm afraid he lacks the killer instinct on the doorstep; I've often thought I should teach him to bite. When he reappeared, it was with a familiar stunted figure in tow: Fifine's proprietor, cap in hand and face like thunder as he saw me reclining by the fire.

Barely had he introduced himself as Monsieur Poilu when he started working himself into a state of high dudgeon, waving his cap in my direction and giving a dramatic performance of a man profoundly wronged. "My precious Fifine," he said, "who is like a daughter to me—madame and I not being blessed with children—has been despoiled, violated, her innocence snatched from her. She is heavy with pup, and I see in this room the lust-crazed scoundrel responsible." In case he hadn't made himself clear, he marched over and pointed at me, finger quivering with passion as he ranted on. "It is he, the beast, and regard the size of him. The thought of that brute and my Fifine, so tiny, so defenseless, *quelle horreur,* her life ruined, and furthermore my lady wife in shock, with already one expensive visit from the doctor, an entire family in despair . . ."

He paused for breath and further inspiration while I reflected on the injustice of it all. Not only was I completely blameless—although it wasn't for lack of trying—but I had actually witnessed the foul deed, and if any innocence had been lost, it certainly was not Fifine's. Little fatty's, more likely. And as I went over the events of that evening, it all became clear to me. Poilu had undoubtedly heard from his friend Roussel about the affair of the overpriced chicken and saw an opportunity here to extract a little financial aid to help with the gynecologist's fees and his wife's migraine tablets, with plenty left over for a good dinner—in other words, a paternity suit. You may think this a cynical conclusion, but I know these people, and I can tell you that they consider the wallet to be one of their vital organs.

Of course, the management had no idea of the truth, and they sat there nodding gravely as Poilu stumbled around the room, clutching his fevered

A paternity suit

brow and frothing at the mouth while he jabbered on about the wages of sin. For a moment, I thought he was going to produce a bill, but he finally ran out of puff and stood glaring at me, manly bosom heaving with emotion, or possibly thirst. Tirades have that effect on some people.

For once, the management didn't resort to the

calming bottle, but started asking him questions. Had he seen the act? When did it take place? Was it not possible that another dog had committed it?

Poilu blustered away, giving the impression that he had been on the spot at the time with his notebook, taking down incriminating details, and then he made the mistake of returning to the subject of Fifine's diminutive size, presumably to encourage more guilt and sympathy among the audience. At last, the management asked the question I'd been waiting for. "How small is Fifine?"

"Ah, but she is tiny, a little nothing, so sweet"— and here Poilu made descriptive motions with his hands, indicating something not much bigger than a well-nourished goldfish.

"In that case," said the management, "how could this unfortunate liaison have been with our dog? As you see, he is large, many times the size of your Fifine, and at least twice her height. These are not the most helpful circumstances."

My sentiments entirely, of course, and as you'll remember, I'd done my level best to overcome natural obstacles without any luck. That settles it, I thought. Game, set, and match to the home team, my good name cleared, and Poilu shown up for the mendacious extortionist I knew he was. I yawned and rolled over, assuming that I'd heard the end of it.

But Poilu didn't leave. He asked for a box, and when the other half fetched an old wine crate from the garage, he set it down on the floor and placed his cap on it. "Now," he said, "please have the kindness to present your dog to the cap."

I don't know who was more puzzled, me or the management, but they decided to humor the old ruffian, and I was brought over to be presented to the cap on the crate. It was more or less in line with my chest, and this seemed to cheer Poilu up enormously. He nodded his head a couple of times and grunted as he circled around me. "It is as I thought," he said. "Imagine that my cap is little Fifine. You will observe that she is now of the same height as your dog, and with this extra elevation, all things are possible. "Yes," he repeated, rubbing his hands with satisfaction, "it is exactly as I thought. Thus was it done."

I could hardly believe my ears, and even the management was finding it difficult to maintain suitably serious expressions. Before we knew it, Poilu would be swearing with hand on heart that he'd seen me creeping around his house carrying a wine crate or a stepladder or a portable hoist, and I'm sure he would have done so if madame hadn't remembered the *rôti de porc* in the oven. She's an even-tempered woman for the most part, but when her cooking is at risk, she can become touchy, which she did. "Bloody nonsense," she said, and sailed off to the kitchen, leaving the other half and Poilu to exchange scowls.

They spend five minutes disagreeing with each other before Poilu realized that it was past his bedtime and that he was unlikely to pick up a check. "This is not the end of the affair," he said. "You will be hearing further from me." And with that, he tossed his curls, rescued his cap, and left.

But we never did hear from him again, and the reason was made clear when Fifine eventually delivered herself of a handful of creatures that only a blind mother could love. I saw them one day when out walking with the other half—gray, potbellied, short-legged runts, the exact image of their father. Case dismissed.

By Their Smell
Shall You Know
Them

*H*ere we go again. There is to be a soirée
tonight, a dinner party, a gathering of cul-
tured and sophisticated people who will
toss epigrams back and forth across the table, keeping the conversational ball in the air. That, at least,
is the optimistic theory. We shall see.

Meanwhile, the management is showing signs of
panic, as is often the case, and watching the pre-
parations is enough to make anyone have second
thoughts about the pleasures of hospitality. A great
deal of wine is brought up from the cellar by the other
half, who amuses himself by making indiscreet comments about the probable effects on those who are
going to drink it. This exasperates madame, by now
in the final throes of a soufflé, and she tells him that
these are our dear friends. The other half snorts and
says he longs to know a teetotaler. Madame snorts

back, and so it goes on. I am made to feel surplus to requirements as far as the kitchen goes. Feet are everywhere, and I find feet very menacing. I withdraw to the safety of the garden to brood.

Why is it that people eat in herds? And when does the habit start? They don't seem to do it when they're small, which is about all you can say in favor of babies. The baby tends to eat alone, and makes a damned messy job of it, too, so there's usually something dropping off the perch. Apart from that, I tend to agree with W. C. Fields. When asked how he liked babies, he replied, "Boiled." Good for him. Unpredictable little monkeys, they are, for the most part, always tweaking your whiskers or trying to unscrew your ears, although I can usually overlook their social failings when the lamb puree starts to fly.

Fortunately, there will be no babies tonight. One knows these things by the disposition of the furniture. When the house is stripped down to resemble an operating theater, you can be sure that Master Baby is coming to call. This hasn't happened, and so tonight we are obviously expecting adults; dangerous, too, in their way, but easier to anticipate.

I dare say it will be the usual zoo once the drink begins to take hold—deafening babble, feet flying with careless abandon, slanderous remarks about close but absent friends, with very little more than the occasional dropped crumb for the silent minority under the table. And some people call the dinner party one of the great pleasures of civilized life. Mind you, the very same people vote for certifiable politicians and enroll in aerobics classes, so you can tell they're a few cards short of a full hand.

Ah, well. All things must pass, and there is always the postmortem to look forward to. It traditionally takes place among the debris in the kitchen, where the other dogs and I gather to enjoy the remains of the feast and the comments of our genial host and hostess as they count the empty bottles and vow never to do it again.

There have been some classic moments, I can tell you—high drama, low comedy, tears and verbal abuse, recriminations and remorse, and even, on one occasion, physical violence. What happened was this.

Mrs. Franklin, a formidable American lady who pays us a visit each year in the course of her stately progress to Cap d'Antibes, had asked to meet a dyed-in-the-wool local, an *homme du coin,* a true native. There was a certain difficulty here, as all natives with any sense lie low in the summer or disappear to somewhere cool and damp like Scotland, where they can wear strange clothes without attracting comment. And so there was much scraping of the bottom of the barrel before the management succeeded in persuading Raoul, the political activist, to leave the barricades of Avignon and grace the table with his unshaven presence.

This was, in its small way, quite a sacrifice, because neither madame nor the other half likes Raoul, who has a spiky disposition to match his chin and drinks like a hole. But the choice was limited, and he was a true native, as he never tired of telling everyone. Not only a true native but also an ardent defender of the purity of the glorious French heritage (which, in my view, consists mainly of museums, arm waving, and a vast amount of organized guzzling, but that's by the way). In any case, Raoul had condescended to put on his least-soiled leather jacket and come, and Mrs. Franklin, wearing her best chintz frock in his honor, was suitably pleased.

They were models of diplomacy during dinner, observing the niceties and professing a deep interest in each other's views about the price of melons and the creeping menace of baseball caps worn backward, and the evening appeared to be doomed to politeness. It was when mine host—whom I suspect of actively encouraging mischief sometimes to keep himself awake—forced brandy down their throats and mentioned Euro Disney that the fur began to fly.

Raoul almost choked on his medicine. *Quelle horreur!* French culture, the shining jewel in civilization's crown, was being debased by unsavory American inventions—*le Coca-Cola, les Big Mac,* and now this unspeakable Mickey Mouse with his prodigious ears. De Gaulle would never have permitted such vulgarity on French soil.

Rubbish, said Mrs. F. Euro Disney has nothing on the Côte d'Azur when it comes to vulgarity. And another thing, she said, topping up her glass, the plumbing works at Euro Disney, which is more than one could say about the rest of France.

Well, you'd have thought she was suggesting that Monsieur Mickey should take up residence in the Elysée Palace. I don't know whether or not Raoul had revered ancestors in the sanitation business, but the reference to plumbing cut him to the quick. He stood up and pounded the table and delivered a force-ten diatribe about the evils of American influence, from chewing gum to Sylvester Stallone (both very popular in France, I might add). And then he made the mistake of moving on, arms all over the place and brandy flying *partout,* to Mrs. Franklin's appearance. "Look at that dress," he said with a curl of the lip, "*that* is what I mean by American vulgarity." He went too far, of course, but you can usually count on Raoul for that, which is why he's not in great demand.

Anyway, that did it. Mrs. Franklin was up and around the table in a flash, moving well for a woman of her years, and caught him squarely on the nose with a right cross from her handbag. It must have contained something heavy—spare jewels for the weekend, perhaps, or half a dozen cans of Mace—because it drew blood. This seemed to encourage her to further efforts, and she chased Raoul from the house, uttering war cries and going for the knockout.

And what, you may ask, did the members of our cultivated audience do while this was taking place? Absolutely nothing, which leads me to believe that the same principle applies to people as to dogs: Never interfere with an honest difference of opinion. He who attempts to intervene gets bitten by both sides.

You will gather from this example that dinner parties in a multiracial society are not without the occasional unplanned diversion, and I'm hoping that tonight's contestants will be a lively bunch.

I hear them arriving now, in full cry even before they get into the house. You've heard donkeys in season, I imagine, all the braying and stamping of feet. It's almost as bad as that. What is worse, they brush by me without so much as a word of greeting. Desperate for drink, I suppose. I go in after them, assessing the ladies' handbags for suitability as offensive weapons, and observe the familiar ritual dance that always precedes serious business.

I still find it peculiar. Men clasp hands and women peck cheeks, but there is never what I would call informative bodily contact. They bend at the waist and bob and duck, but they fail to get to grips, if you follow me. There's no substance to the exchange. How can you hope to discover anything of interest from an arm's-length handshake or a brief contact just west of the earrings?

My greeting methods, on the other hand, are genuinely cordial, or so I like to think, and extremely revealing. When approaching, I wag the tail with vigor. This reassures the more timid souls, induces an immediate sense of bonhomie, and prepares the

My greeting methods

way for a more intimate salute—a probing sniff to the
guest's central area. I should say here that my height
enables me to accomplish this without any of the
servile hopping up and down that dogs of reduced
stature are obliged to perform. You've seen them,
I'm sure, looking like furry yo-yos.

So here we are, snout to groin. Gasps and squeals
from the ladies, and manly attempts by the gentlemen to treat the encounter as another quaint facet of
bucolic life. "Boys will be boys," they say. Or, with a
trace of apprehension, "Does he bite?" I must say
I've been tempted to take a mouthful from time to

time, particularly when they call me Rover or spill
gin on my head, but so far I've managed to hold
myself back. There'll come a day, though. There are
limits even to my good nature.

This initial investigation takes only a few seconds,
but it can be very informative for those of us with an
educated nose and an appreciation of ethnic differences. Tonight, as I make my rounds, I find that we
have a mixed bag of suspects from several countries,
and it's interesting how often their personal bou-
quets conform to national stereotypes.

Here we have Jeremy, the Englishman, fitting the
profile perfectly. He smells damp, with undertones
of sherry and residual hints of ancient tweeds
and unsuccessful dandruff shampoo. Despite the
warmth of the evening, he wears thick trousers that
bring to mind autumn and rough shooting. He calls
me "dear boy," and he seems rather disappointed
when I withdraw my nose to move on.

Jules and Jim, the antique dealers from the village,
are capering around in their usual excitable fashion.
They, like most of our compatriots, are invariably
pungent: piercing eau de cologne mingling with the
aftereffects of a powerfully seasoned lunch—garlic, of
course, with considerable assistance from anchovies
and peppercorns, and a faint souvenir of aniseed and
licorice left over from the breakfast pastis. A combination that often makes me sneeze all over their white
espadrilles.

Young Linda and her sister Erica from Washington, smelling as all Americans do. They remind me of some newly laundered shirts that I once toyed with in an idle moment. There is also a whiff of mouthwash. I seldom linger with Americans, because of their sanitary bouquet. Besides, I have a feeling that many of them regard me as a health hazard.

Finally, we have the venerable Angus, an old friend of the management from the western Highlands. I live in hope that he will one day turn up in kilt and sporran, which would be a new experience for both of us. Tonight, sadly, he is festooned in antique corduroy, and he smells, as usual, of groats, spilled whisky, Border terriers, and cigar ash.

And that is the cast of characters for this evening. Will they lock horns and revive the old traditions of verbal assault and battery? I hope so, because I have found that when passions run high, there is a fine, free carelessness with the hands, and food tends to drop off the table as a result.

Eventually, after honking at each other for an hour or so, madame sounds the bugle, and the guests go in for dinner. Before joining them, I tidy up the canapés that some kind spirit has left for me on a low table and reflect on the aromatic diversity of the world's human population. I look forward with interest to meeting my first Australian.

The Sitting

*P*eople have many puzzling habits—dieting, ballroom dancing, stamp collecting, and a touching faith in the stock market, to name just a few—but one of the most curious is their reluctance to take advantage of the pleasures of a simple walk. At least once a day, the management and I set off in search of exercise and adventure in the forest. Kind and thoughtful of them, I dare say, although there are times when I'd be happier in front of the fire. But they seem to enjoy it, and so I always show willing. The forest's a big place, after all, and I wouldn't want them to get lost.

But what still surprises me after all these years is their lack of initiative. All they do is trudge along— no sniffing, no carefree rolling, no chasing of chickens, no stops to sprinkle one's bounty at the base of trees, no ritual burials, no ambushes, no digging, and very little in the way of leaping nimbly from crag to crag. I try to encourage them by example, but they are set in their ways and resistant to training. It could be age, of course. You can't teach an old human new tricks.

Anyway, it was during one of these expeditions that a chance encounter led to my brief career in the world of art. Let my story be a warning to you that no good deed goes unpunished.

We were in the hills above the village, the management trailing along in the rear, as usual, when I heard sounds of movement, and I burst through the bushes to investigate, hoping for a rabbit. To my disappointment, all I saw was a human figure, and one that I recognized. It was Eloise, the artist, drifting through the glades like a lost weekend, taking photographs of twigs. She was wearing her watercolorist's ensemble of flowing garment, tapestry thong sandals with matching camera strap, and picturesque hat. Doubtless, she was looking for inspiration, which has eluded her for several years to my certain knowledge. She greeted me with a coo of delight.

"Oooh, *c'est magnifique*," she said. "Stay just where you are, framed in the greenery like something out of Le Douanier Rousseau. So *sauvage*." And with that, she took a photograph of me. I had a strand of wild honeysuckle clinging to one ear, I remember, and that must have set her off. They're an odd lot, artists, prone to whimsy.

The management came struggling through the undergrowth, and they and Eloise kissed and flapped hands as if they hadn't met for years. In fact, she's always over at the house, probably to see if she's left her muse behind in a corner somewhere, but when friends come across one another unexpectedly, they tend to make a meal of it. Don't ask me why. Anyway, I was about to follow an interesting and gamy scent—a fox, it might have been, or possibly old Roussel exerting himself—when I was stopped in my tracks by something Eloise was saying to the management.

It had come to her in a flash, she said, clutching her hat with excitement, when she saw me appear in the bushes. It was a high-concept moment, a blinding spasm of inspiration; the scales had fallen from her eyes and now the path ahead was clear.

The management nodded and shuffled their feet politely, but I could tell they were just as bewildered as I was until Eloise went on to explain herself. She's not too good at that, actually, so I'll give you a shortened interpretation of the ten minutes of gibberish that followed. Apparently, she had been planning a definitive series of watercolors of cobwebs—hence the camera and the twig photography, for research purposes—but somehow the work hadn't been flowing. It rarely does, if the truth be known. Eloise is what might be called an artist in waiting, rather than a practicing painter. My own view is that she's happier like that. The hours are shorter, for one thing, and your social life doesn't suffer.

But now, as a result of the revelation in the bushes, she had decided to abandon the cobweb project, toss aside her watercolors, and embrace canvas and oils— the bones and blood, as she said, of the mature and serious artist. You have to know her, really, to appreciate the unconscious humor of that remark, but that's how she put it. The management continued to nod and shuffle and keep straight faces while they waited for the lecturer to leave Cézanne and Picasso and return to the point.

After one or two brief excursions into Fauvism and the influence of absinthe on van Gogh's work, our lady of the palette finally revealed her plan. It was to create a masterpiece, a life-size study of the king of the forest springing from a bush, the epitome of nature in its untamed magnificence. Well, I'm normally not slow to get the drift of a conversation, but I must say it took a few seconds before I realized exactly what she was babbling about. She wanted to paint a portrait of me.

Mixed emotions came into play here. On the one hand, there was a gratifying recognition of my heroic qualities, the chance to be immortalized, and possibly a few bones on the side by way of model's refreshments. On the other hand, I had misgivings about the painter. When I tell you that this is a woman

The chance to be immortalized

whom I have heard admitting that she has serious artistic problems every morning with her choice of lipstick, you can imagine what was going through my mind. We would be dithering away for years in the studio, life would pass me by, and by the time the portrait was finished—that is, if it was ever started— I'd be old enough to require the assistance of a registered nurse to help me lift my leg.

The management, however, had no such fears. I think they had visions of my likeness hanging in the

Louvre, in the livestock section next to those over-weight medieval cherubs everyone seems to admire so much. Their Boy, cheek by jowl with the old masters. They thought the idea was thrilling. A dangerous thing, enthusiasm, particularly if Eloise is involved. But I'm getting ahead of myself.

The conference in the forest adjourned, with Eloise rushing off in search of her portrait painter's kit and the management speculating optimistically about the completion date of the great work. My own estimate was a good eighteen months, and that was just to buy the materials, so I didn't give the matter much thought over the next few days. It would never happen, I was sure, and to be honest, I was relieved. I'm not cut out for still life.

Ah, well. None of us is infallible. To my great surprise, I was wrong, and Eloise called a week later to say that she was ready for the first sitting. I was far from pleased, as I'd made plans for the day and, as I've said, had doubts about the whole project. But the management was in a state of high excitement, and for their sake, I was misguided enough to cooperate. After some quite unnecessary primping and combing of the whiskers, I was delivered to the door of what Eloise likes to refer to as her "atelier."

It was at the bottom of her garden, a long, narrow building that had been converted—quite recently, judging by the smell—from a convalescent home for goats. And there in the doorway was the modern answer to Stubbs and Rembrandt, decked out in full combat uniform. Gone were the sandals, flowing garment, and floppy hat of her dabbling days in watercolors. This was a new and dedicated Eloise, dressed in what looked like welder's overalls and rubber boots, with a vermilion bandeau around her head.

She led me inside, chattering on, artist to model, about working together for the greater glory of the painted image while I made a tour of the premises. I'd never been in an artist's studio before, and so it was all new to me. A large blank canvas was on an easel in the middle of the room; next to it, a long table with tubes of paint, pots full of brushes, palettes, and—indispensable to all great artists, I remember thinking—a telephone. And in front of the easel was what I can best describe as an artificial grotto.

There were rocks, tastefully arranged to form an uneven base, with a variety of dying shrubs wedged in the crevices. If you had a vivid imagination and an uncritical eye, you might have detected some distant resemblance to nature, but I was unconvinced. However, I did notice that some biscuits had been left on one of the rocks, and I dealt with them while I listened to Eloise making a phone call. Then she made another, and another, and each time it was the same story. She was calling her friends to tell them not to disturb her—ironic, really, given her talent for interrupting herself at every opportunity. But she sent out the message that an important commission had been undertaken, artist in the throes of creation, no contact with the outside world until further notice, and so on. I wondered how the old masters had managed without phones. Messengers with cleft sticks, I imagine.

I was becoming a little restive by this time, feeling more than ever that my obliging nature had let me in for an extended dose of tedium. Remember what I said about good deeds? One pays for them, there's no doubt about it, and as I gazed out of the window to the accompaniment of yet another phone call, I almost regretted being born with such a distinguished appearance. I'm quite happy for artists to suffer for their art, but I wish they'd leave us models out of it.

Finally, Eloise put aside the phone and battle commenced. She took me over to install me in the grotto and made numerous adjustments before she succeeded in placing me in a position of acute discomfort. This was my pose, so she told me, and I was not to move, a rock up the backside notwithstanding. She stepped back, extended an arm, cocked her thumb, and squinted at me thoughtfully, in the manner of Degas getting a grip on perspective. But no. It wouldn't do. Something was missing. I was allowed to stand at ease while she went out to the garden to look for whatever it was.

Back she came in triumph, holding an armful of weeds. Horticulture isn't one of my strong points, so I can't give you their name, but I'm sure you've come across them. They grow in curling tendrils, and they stick to you like long strands of burrs. They're the devil to get off, so you keep well clear of them if you have any sense. Eloise, of course, doesn't qualify.

She began draping this dreadful stuff around my head and shoulders, mumbling some claptrap about a verdant garland completing the effect. By the time she'd finished, I felt completely ridiculous, as you would if someone dressed you up as a bush. But Eloise was obviously convinced we were making progress, and she pushed me back on my jagged perch with exclamations of artistic delight. "Yes," she said, "yes. I can see it now, that head framed by a symbol of nature's fertility. *Superbe.*" Personally, I could see very little through the foliage hanging over my brow, and I put that forward as the cause of the accident. It wasn't malice aforethought, despite what she said later.

So far, not a drop of paint had been spilled in earnest. I was uncomfortable at both ends, three-quarters blind, and rapidly running out of patience. And then the phone rang.

Would Picasso have answered it, or any of those maestros of the brush? Of course not. Did Eloise? Of course she did. I have heard it said—unkind, I know, as the truth often is—that it would take surgery to remove a phone from her ear, and she was settling down to a detailed discussion of the benefits of lipo-suction with one of her weight-conscious friends when I decided that enough was enough. I rose from my bed of pain and went toward the door, with the intention of disentangling myself from my leafy disguise. Unfortunately, vision being impaired, I bumped into the easel, the canvas came down on my head, and a combination of instinct and irritation made me fight back.

It was the redeeming moment of the day. I don't know if you've ever had reason to attack a four-by-four canvas, but if you're ever feeling out of sorts, I can't recommend it too highly. It rips like a dream, and there's no chance of personal injury. I was at it

The redeeming moment of the day

like a tiger, until nothing remained but strips and fragments, with a distraught Eloise giving a hysterical running commentary to her friend on the phone. "He has turned into a vicious killer. My work is destroyed. I fear for my life. Call the police." I should add that by now the terrified artist had climbed to a position of safety on top of her table, her booted feet causing havoc among the tubes of aquamarine and madder, some of which spurted out and landed on me.

I'm sure you can guess the rest. An emergency call summoned the management, they hurried over, and, do you know, it was the first time I'd ever seen them flinch. There I was, festooned with weeds and morsels of canvas, decorated with multicolored blobs of paint, and pawing at the door to get out, with Eloise up on the table, clutching the phone to her breast and preparing to swoon. I wasn't in the best position to appreciate the sight myself, but I'm sure some people would have paid a modest entrance fee.

It ended badly for us all. The management promised a check in the post by return, to compensate for general wear and tear. I was subjected to a disagreeable session with scissors and paint stripper. And Eloise was in shock, so she said, for months afterward. So much for art. Not worth the fuss, if you ask me.

Notes on the Human Species

If I live to be sixteen, I shall never fully understand the rich complexities of human nature.
Not sure that I want to, either. It would be a lifetime's work, and brooding over the mysteries of
existence is bad for your health. Look what happens
to philosophers. Most of them end up barking mad,
taking to the bottle, or becoming professors of exis-
tentialism at obscure universities.

Having said that, I won't deny that after many
happy years of living with the management and their
occasionally suspect friends, I have come to certain
conclusions about the beast with two legs. Flashes of
insight have occurred, as they will if you observe
closely, keep your mouth shut and your ears open.
Instructive moments stay in the memory, adding to
the store of knowledge. Take, for example, the day I
learned about the sanctity of the human infant.

It happened during that socially perilous period after dinner, when those around the table are often tempted to let fly with a juicy indiscretion, or even— *in vino veritas*—to tell the truth. They often regret it the next day, and remorseful phone calls are exchanged. But by then, fortunately, it's too late.

On the evening in question, we were privileged to have the company of an earth mother. She had three young children, and never let anyone forget it— photographs with the cocktails, fascinating tales of their exploits with bib and rattle during the first course, followed by up-to-date reports, in great and unnecessary detail, of the number of teeth and their experiments with bodily functions. I found it hard to take, and I wasn't trying to eat, but she pressed on regardless while the other guests did as best they could to choke down the roast lamb. Finally, having run out of hard news, she put forward the offensive theory that people have dogs as child substitutes. Misguided and discourteous, of course, but hardly original, and I thought the remark would receive the lack of attention it deserved.

I hadn't reckoned, however, on the effect of her monologue on the other half. I may have mentioned previously that it usually takes something close to an earth tremor to rouse him from his after-dinner reverie. But at this point—inspired, no doubt, by a surfeit of propaganda on the joys of fertility—he pricked up his ears and bit back. Good stuff it was, too, the gist of it being that many couples in these

He picked up his ears and bit back.

overcrowded times live in small apartments where dogs are forbidden. Desperate for companionship, the couple either buys a parakeet or has a baby, depending on available cage space. Therefore, one could just as easily put forward the opposite argument—that children are, in fact, dog substitutes. Have another drink.

The other half has found himself in trouble before because of his frivolous attitude to sacred cows, but seldom have I seen such a dramatic response. Vibrating with emotion like a blancmange in heat, the earth mother fixed him with furious and incandescent eye. "That's outrageous," said she. "Are you seriously comparing my little Tommy with a parakeet?"

A hush fell upon the table while everyone waited for the other half to extricate himself from the situation. But the devil was in him that night, and he wasn't in a mood to appease. "Why not?" said he. "They're both small. They're both noisy. They both spill their food. And they both have difficulty controlling their bowels." All true, of course, but not really what a mother wants to hear.

And it was enough to conclude the evening's entertainment. The offended party threw down her napkin, picked up the family album, and dragged her husband off into the night, complaining loudly about insults to motherhood and swearing never to speak to that dreadful man again. "What a relief," the other half was heard to mutter, which caused him to be banished to do penance in the kitchen. I kept my head well down. I'd enjoyed every minute of it, of course, but it doesn't do to gloat.

Musing on events in my basket after lights out, my thoughts turned to other sensitive issues where unfashionable opinions or a few words spoken in jest can lead to alarm and despondency and ruptured social ties. There are many touchy subjects, when you come to think about it, from politics—which I gather many people still take seriously—to the role of the condom in modern society. I've listened to overheated discussions about both, and I've seen normally mild-mannered, reasonable people behave like ferrets in a sack over the most minor disagreements. They like to win, you see, and they get cross if they don't. There's nothing as strange as folk.

It was with this in mind that I spent a few days reviewing the thoughts collected in the preceding pages—to be certain I'd included all that might be of interest to posterity, or anyone else, for that matter. To my surprise, I found that I might have neglected my own kind. What of the youthful and untried among us, ignorant of human ways, cast adrift in a strange world where people relieve themselves indoors and punish the dog who imitates them? Logic doesn't answer; only experience does. And so I offer these hints. Random *pensées,* they may be, but none the worse for that. See what you think.

Advice to the Young Dog

1. Beware of Christmas. It is traditionally a time when puppies are brought into the happy home as gifts. If they manage to survive an early diet of turkey, mince pies, liqueur chocolates, wrapping paper, tinsel, and tree ornaments, they grow, as puppies do. For some reason, this causes astonishment and consternation among the older members of the family, who should have known better. But they don't, and by spring they're looking for someone prepared to take over a dog that has become an inconvenience. Christmas puppies should not make long-term plans. Sad but true.

2. Do not even attempt to understand the lure of television. I like to think of myself as fairly sophisticated, able to move freely among different social groups, sympathetic to their interests, however bizarre, and so forth. But here I am baffled. A box

filled with small and noisy people, a disagreeable
scent of heated plastic, the room plunged into darkness, conversation banned, and the faint sounds of
snoring in the background—is this enjoyable? I can't
make head or tail of it myself. Have you ever seen
rabbits hypnotized by flashlight? That's television,
as far as I'm concerned. For drama and entertainment, give me ants any day.

3. You may one night be disturbed by the stealthy
arrival through a window of gentlemen who tiptoe
around the house in silence. These are burglars.
Never bark at them. They have no respect for animal
rights and can be violent. Postpone making any noise
until they are safely out of the house. With luck, they
might have taken the television.

4. The etiquette of bathing confused me for several
months, but the rules seem to be as follows. It is acceptable for people to immerse themselves in water
every day; indeed, they consider it a virtue and a joy.
They sing; they play games with the soap; they
emerge pink and glowing and pleased with themselves. Seeing this, the novice dog who wishes to
please may be tempted to follow their example by
taking a refreshing squirm in a puddle. This is not
acceptable. Neither is shaking oneself dry in the living room or cleaning the facial hair with a brisk rub
on the carpet. As in most aspects of life, a dual
standard operates here, and it doesn't favor those of
us with four legs and a muddy gusset.

5. Learn to distinguish between natural friends

and natural enemies. I always warm to gardeners (because we have a mutual interest in digging), clumsy eaters, those who understand the principles of bribery to ensure good behavior, and denture wearers, who find biscuits difficult. To be treated with caution: anyone dressed in white, people who make patronizing inquiries about your pedigree, grumpy old men with sticks, and vegetarians (except at mealtimes when there is meat on the table that they wish to dispose of discreetly). To be avoided: women who carry photographs of their cats. They are beyond hope.

6. Recognize the need for selective obedience. Under normal circumstances, you can do more or less what you like. Man's innate idleness and short attention span will save you from too much discipline. But there will be moments of crisis when it pays to respond to a call from the authorities. You can always tell. Voices are raised, hysteria looms, and threats are uttered. When they shout in capital letters—as in "BOY! DAMNIT!"—return to base immediately, pretending you didn't hear the first time. Wag sincerely, and all will be well.

7. Do not bring friends of the opposite sex home. This will only encourage indelicate speculation about your intentions, and it may lead to a period of house arrest. Romance, in my view, is best conducted on neutral ground, where you're unlikely to find yourself cornered and you can retain what is known these days as "maximum deniability." Follow

the example of our eminent leaders: Admit to nothing until your accusers have you by the short hairs.

8. Never bite vets, even when attacked from behind by a chilly thermometer. They mean well.

9. Finally, remember that we live in an imperfect world. People make mistakes. Cocktail parties, pale-colored furniture, hair transplants, New Year's Eve, worming tablets, vibrant orange Lycra, diamanté dog collars, jogging, grooming, telephone sex, leg waxing—the list is long, and life is short. My advice is to make the best of it, and to make allowances. To err is human. To forgive, canine.

To err is human. To forgive, canine.

Anyone for a walk?

Anything Considered

BY PETER MAYLE

From the author of the national bestsellers *A Year in Provence* and *Toujours Provence* comes a rollicking caper set in the south of France. A British ex-pat living in the Cote d'Azur, Bennett has abandoned an advertising career and found little to replace it. Devilishly charming and a bit roguish, he has a champagne taste but a beer bankroll.

An offer from a wealthy businessman involves Bennett in a promising scheme to corner the truffle market in France. Soon Bennett finds himself living a life in Monaco to which he always wanted to become accustomed (including, of course, mouth-watering meals). However, there are complications in the form of the Corsican and Sicilian mafias. And, by the end, a beautiful New York woman, wine-making monks, *gendarmes* working at cross-purposes, a few colorful goons, and the inevitable French village gossips will all play a role in the satisfying denouement.

Fiction/0-679-44123-9

Available in hardcover from Alfred A. Knopf
at your local bookstore, or call toll-free to order:
1-800-793-2665 (credit cards only).